L♥VE

and KNISHES

An Irrepressible Guide
to Jewish Cooking

Sara Kasdan

Illustrated by Louis Slobodkin

ALEXANDER BOOKS

Publisher: Ralph Roberts
Cover Design: WorldComm®
Executive Editor: Kathryn L. Hall

Interior Design & Electronic Page Assembly: WorldComm®

Photo of Sara Kasdan by Moseley Photography, Bob Gardner.

10 9 8 7 6 5 4 3 2 1
Second Edition

ISBN 1-57090-004-3

Library of Congress: 94-072056

Alexander Books—a division of Creativity, Inc.—is a full-service publisher located at 65 Macedonia Road, Alexander NC 28701. Phone (704) 252-9515 or (704) 255-8719 fax.

Alexander Books is distributed to the trade by Associated Publishers Group, 1501 County Hospital Road, Nashville, Tennessee 37218. Telephone (800) 327-5113. Fax (615) 254-2405.

LOVE AND KNISHES

*If the way to a man's heart is
through his stomach, then knishes
will get there faster ...
and stay longer.*

Glossary

KREPLECH: Chinese definition: *Won Ton*; Italian definition: *Ravioli*.

LOX: A partner to bagels.

MECHIAH (kitchen version): Someone else doing the dishes.

MESHUGE: Just plain crazy.

MESHUGY: Crazy, Southern style.

MILCHIKS: Foods made with dairy products. What you serve when you don't feel like cooking and you're tired of delicatessen.

MITZVAH: A good deed, like taking the cook out to dinner once in awhile. In some cases, this *mitzvah* is a two—way good deed; she's enjoying and you're getting a good dinner for a change.

NICHT GEFEHRLICH: Not so terrible. So what if the cake did fall! Let 'em eat bread!

SCHLIMAZEL (kitchen version): The unfortunate cook whose children run through the kitchen banging doors just when the cake is in the oven.

SCHLIMIEHL (kitchen version): The cook who, when the cake is in the oven, runs through the kitchen herself, banging doors.

SCHMALTZ: Rendered chicken or poultry fat used for frying or seasoning (see page 48). In many cases, shortening may be substituted, just as a muskrat coat may be substituted for a mink.

ZEI GEZUNDT (kitchen version): You cook it your way, I'll cook it mine.

❤ CONTENTS ❤

5 Milchiks Is Milchiks 37

6 Put Some Schmaltz in it 47

7 So From Hunger You Won't Starve 49

13 Education Is a Wonderful Thing   89

14 Papa Called It Grass   99

15 And It Came to Passover   103

... 35 Years Later

You don't have to be Jewish to enjoy good food and laughter. You'll find them both in *Love and Knishes* ... and more ... a bit of the folkways of the Jewish people.

For 33 years *Love and Knishes* gave this to its several hundred thousand readers (buyers and borrowers). To Jewish readers it gave memories of Mama and Papa. Nobody could cook like Mama—the wholesome daily food and the delicious traditional dishes for religious holidays. Did she put a pinch of suger in the gefilte fish or no? What wonderful things did she put in the strudel? ("Don't eat! I made for company!") Jewish women wanted to learn to cook these dishes like their mothers did and to pass this knowledge on to their children and their children's children, but they couldn't. The publisher had retired.

With the rebirth of *Love and Knishes* with help from Alexander Books, I hope that the food, the humor and mores unique to Jewish culture can be enjoyed by a new generation.

ACKNOWLEDGMENTS

To my many friends, in many places, who so graciously shared with me their family recipes, I wish to express my deep appreciation.

My thanks to the Embassy of Israel for the Israeli recipes;

To Sam Levenson for his mother's recipe for *gehakte leber*;

To Cissy Gregg, home consultant, *Louisuille Courier-Journal*, for help and advice;

To Irene Conn, for her gracious assistance;

To Dr. Israel Naamani, director of the Bureau of Jewish Education, Louisville, Kentucky;

To Harvey Curtis Webster, Professor of English, University of Louisville—but you positively shouldn't think he is helping me with the English;

To Lucille Jones Webster, for nagging and proofreading;

To Mary Baxter and Barbara Rehm for proofreading.

To the folks at Alexander Books for bringing *Love and Knishes* back to life for the delight of more generations.

❤ I ❤

YOU SHOULD LIVE SO LONG!

One day it comes to me the idea to write a Jewish cookbook. Why? Who can say? Thousands of cooks there are with good Jewish backgrounds. They don't need to cook from a book; they can cook from their heads. So why should I write a book? On the other hand, why not? There are plenty of cooks whose background is still ahead of them. They remember the wonderful food that mama and grandmama made and they want to make it, too. And if they don't remember, their husbands do, which is even worse. Good food is to eat, not just to remember.

Also a reason: I am the type person who likes to study human nature. While I am studying human nature, I am learning one thing for sure—that everybody, no matter who he is, likes to eat good food. Jewish food is good food, so why shouldn't everybody like to eat it, even if he is not Jewish? Besides, by eating other people's food, you are learning about them and it is bringing you closer together. Farther apart it is not driving you, anyway.

We live in a world with different people, so we want to know them better, and to know them better by eating their type of food is like killing two birds with one stone. You are knowing someone better, and it is at the same time a pleasure. So if you are not Jewish, this book will bring you pleasure, I hope, because this is my intention.

To start a book, first of all you have to have a title, so I'm studying other cookbooks to learn what to name mine. First of all, I'm learning that it isn't enough one title; you must also have a subtitle. For instance, one book is called *Victor Schmorgesborge: A Guide to Danish Cooking,* another is called *Behind the Iron Samovar: A Guide to Russian Cooking,* and so on and so forth. So I am calling my book *Love and Knishes: A Guide to Jewish Cooking,* but if you think this book will lead you to the fine art of Jewish cooking, you should live so long!

This is not because I have *not* tried to be exact in all my measurements and directions ... I have, but that is just the point: The true art of Jewish cooking is based on inexactness. Don't believe everything you read. If it says "add a tablespoon of butter," does it hurt if you put in two spoons? What could be bad? If one spoon is good, so two is better. Why not, if you can afford it? And if you are making strudel, does it hurt to put in a little extra in the filling? Besides the apples, nuts, raisins, coconut, preserves, cinnamon, and sugar, Mama would put in a few gumdrops. Did it kill us? So the bride is too beautiful. Some fault!

Some people think it is impossible to get from a Jewish cook a recipe, like, God forbid, it should fall into strange hands. It's impossible to get, yes, but because it is such a secret? No. You couldn't be more wrong.

A true Jewish cook, who, having stuffed you with her creations, says, "So take a little more ... enjoy," and when you tell her you are under doctor's orders to reduce, she replies, "Diet, shmiet ... so long as you're healthy," would be only too happy to give you her recipe. So where is the secret, so where? The secret is that this modern generation has gone to college—so how can you teach them how to cook? You've got to put it into their heads by the level teaspoon yet. If you tell them, "Put in a little flour," so they ask you "How much?" and when you say, "Put in 'til it looks right," so do they know what you are talking about?

Can an artist measure out a masterpiece? If I should say to Mr. Rembrandt, "Paint for me a picture. You should use only one level teaspoon blue and seven–eighths cup green" ... so from this you're not getting a Mona Lisa.

When you go to college, you can cook only from a book. It is true, my Mama paid lip service to those who cooked from books. So what can you do if you eat in a person's house? Can you say, "Pheh! poison! You can't even take it to your mouth!"? Of course not. You say, "Ei, yi, yi, yi, such a *maichel* (delicacy) ... you must got it from a book." And you wipe your lips and go home.

Now, Mama was a good cook. For 50 years, once a year, she made strudel, the best in the world, but she herself never knew exactly how she did it. Every time she worried if the strudel would come out right. This added spice to an otherwise quiet existence. For years, I wanted to learn how to make strudel. So why didn't I watch her and learn? If I watched, she would get flustered and ruin the strudel. Who could afford to take such a chance?

This may give you some idea of the trouble I had collecting recipes. At first, I thought, "So why should I kill myself going from house to house collecting recipes? I'll bring to my house all the good cooks. I'll serve a little something and they will give me recipes." So good already.

They come to my house ... one woman brings even a purse full of recipes carefully clipped from a Yiddish–language newspaper. "This is a gold mine," I thought. After reading the recipes, I thought, "This is a gold mine?" They read: "Retzipe ... how you make Southern fried chicken. Retzipe ... how you make chocolate–chip cookies."

A fine end to Jewish cooking! But, after all, why should the newspaper waste space telling Jewish cooks how to cook Jewish food? They could tell the newspaper. So I went on asking for recipes. I asked one at a time. How can you ask one cook when ten others are sitting by? Mrs. C. starts on a recipe. "*Zei gezundt*," says Mrs. B. Now, literally translated, "*zei gezundt*" means "you should be well," but in this instance and similar ones, it means, "Mrs. C., mind your own business. You think you can cook! My enemies should know from cooking like you know. In mine, I put lemon ..."

I have come to the conclusion that a good Jewish cook must cook by taste, so my advice to you is to find a Jewish friend ... or make one (this is easy; tell her only that you hear she is the best cook in town) and get yourself invited to dinners. Once you know how the food should taste, you can start out with *Love and Knishes* and go on from there.

But if you can get yourself invited to dinners, so why should you wear yourself out cooking? So give up already. Send *Love and Knishes* to a friend.

❤ 2 ❤

ALL I DO IS PUSH
A BUTTON

This chapter is to show you how modern I was when I was modern, which was maybe 1956 when I was writing the book for the first time ... So today I'm not so modern. With a computer I'm not cooking. With my memory and my heart I'm cooking. ...

Some women make such a to–do about housework like it was hard work or something. Not me. If you are smart ... and you have money ... so it's easy. Take me, for instance.

All I do is push a button. I've got an automatic washer, an automatic dryer, and a well–nourished garbage dispos–all. In America is a regular push–button civilization.

Nowadays we've got it easy. We've got leisure. In fact, so much leisure we've got that it is sometimes easier to work than to find out what to do with the leisure. Some of my friends join clubs with their leisure—the Ladies Auxiliary, the Benevolent Society, Hadassah; before they know it, they are on "the board" ... an honor, why not? Before they know it, they are working so hard on the board that they fire their maids so they should have the excuse to tell the president they have to do all their own housework so they must resign; so finally, they have leisure again.

I've got one friend who was having trouble with her leisure. "I'm getting bored," she tells me. "I don't know what to do with myself." Now, Mama always had an answer for that. "You don't know what to do ... so go hit your head on the wall." But my friend is living in a modern apartment ... the neighbors wouldn't like it. So I tell her, "You're bored? So go bake a cake." And do you know what? From this idea, my friend has already a national chain of bakeries and is thinking of opening a branch office in South America.

Nu, this is neither here nor there. I was saying that all I do is push a button. But do you think I'm happy with only a washer, dryer, ironer, mixer, vacuum, dishwasher, and garbage dispos–all? Not hardly. The dream of my life is to have an electric stove. So I'm blessed by God. I live to see the day when I get an electric stove.

One day I look out of my picture window in my new one–floor–plan ranch–type house in the suburbs and I see a big truck. "The Automatic–Automatic Stove Co., Inc." is printed on the side. Who could be so happy? At last I will set eyes on my new electric stove. That's right—I never saw it before. You see, I've got a friend who has a friend who sells wholesale, but he doesn't like he should be bothered by individual customers who are just looking, so my friend orders for me wholesale over the phone.

Now, when I see the truck driver, I'm taking him gently by the hand and I'm leading him into my new pine–paneled kitchen. "Here," I say, "here is where I want the stove."

"Sidewalk delivery," says he.

"Mr. Deliveryman," I say, "what do you mean sidewalk delivery? Sidewalks I haven't. I'm living now in the country. What's the matter, the union won't let you take it into the kitchen?" Right away I'm getting anti–labor.

"All right, then," says he, "roadside delivery."

You think he doesn't mean it? He means it. So my stove is standing for days while I'm looking for a union it should have jurisdiction to come into the kitchen. Eventually, I find.

"So uncrate," I say. "Connect."

"Uncrate, yes. Connect, no." For connecting I need an appliance man. So try and find. Find you can, but they should come out and connect a stove you bought from someone else, no. "From whom did you buy it, from whom?" they ask. So can I tell them I took from them the business? They tell me I should go where I got it ... they'll connect.

Eventually, I'm losing my temper and when they are asking from whom did I get it and getting ready to tell me to go back there, I say, "I got it from the devil. Does it hurt you?" The appliance man, being a gentleman, and because I'm paying him double, connects.

So this is the story how I lived to get an electric stove. Such a stove! Three ovens. For a while I couldn't figure out why three ovens, then it comes to me clear. The Automatic–Automatic Co. is not anti–Semitic. They've got an oven for *milchiks* (dairy dishes), an oven for *flaishiks* (meats), and the third? Naturally, that is for *trefe* (nonkosher). After all, they have gentile customers, too.

The stove has a deep–well cooker, a french–fryer, a griddle, three thermostats (you shouldn't make too hot the ovens), a clock, a timer, three outlets (you should connect the toaster, the percolator, and the vacuum cleaner), bells they should ring when it's over the cooking, and forty-eight push buttons, all colors, with lights yet. This is a stove? This is a Christmas tree ... with presents.

The stove comes with a guarantee and questions you should answer they should know how you like it. So I answer the questions.

"Was your last range electric?"

"No, before, I'm cooking with gas."

"Why did you choose the Automatic–Automatic in preference to other ranges?"

"Because I'm getting it wholesale."

"Do you like the wonderful new push–button feature?"

"Why not? If progress says push buttons, so I'll learn to push."

"Do you like the range because it is so clean?"

Why shouldn't it be clean? All day long, I'm cleaning the stove. You think I'll let my new stove it should get dirty? It's coming apart piece by piece, and piece by piece I'm cleaning and putting back together. Sometimes I think I'll buy a little gas burner I should have leisure to look at my stove and enjoy.

Sometimes I have a little trouble with the buttons. Such buttons! Beauties they are ... not buttons. In neat rows: pink, blue, red, green, purple, orange, and colors I don't even know the names yet. For such a stove you need to go to college.

Every morning I stand in front of the stove. I stretch my left arm forward, my right arm back. You think I'm doing this for my health? Never. I'm just setting myself up I should push the correct button—left front, right rear.

Sometimes I find a burner red–hot while the food sits and waits on an unlit burner. Sometimes I turn on the oven to come back an hour later and find it cold. Why? Instead of pushing the bake–it–right–now button, I pushed the bake-it-later-while-I'm-at-the-Sisterhood-meeting button.

Sometimes, I put down a glass bowl on a burner which it should be cold but isn't, and I don't need the bells should ring to tell me when to come back to the kitchen. When pieces of glass are flying all over the kitchen, so they ring their own bells.

We never eat on time any more. I've got to cook with in one hand a cookbook I shouldn't make mistakes with the recipes, and in the other hand an instruction book I shouldn't make mistakes with the stove. From two books I'm cooking now.

So why don't I go back to cooking with gas? Crazy I'd have to be. By my father I never had such a stove. I'm the envy of all my friends, and from my enemies I'm not even talking.

Because it's still an old habit, I'm keeping on the stove a box of matches. Anyway, who knows what can happen with the electricity? It's always best to be prepared.

Maybe you think I don't believe in my stove and all the wonderful things that can happen in this world? You couldn't be more wrong. My heart tells me that someday, some golden day, I will push the right combination of buttons and from my stove will come rolling out knishes and strudel and honey cake without end. Someday, my heart tells me, I'm hitting the jackpot.

❤ 3 ❤

IT SHOULDN'T HAPPEN LIKE IT HAPPENS

It shouldn't happen like it happens, but sometimes a friend gets sick. So it is positively your duty to do something about it. Why should you sit there and let her die without your help? It is not only your duty, it's a *mitzvah*. Now, a *mitzvah* is something that Boy Scouts are supposed to do every day—the good deed that paves the way to heaven. The way some good Jewish women rush to perform a *mitzvah*, you would think, God forbid, they weren't so sure of getting to heaven. They are regular Mitzvah Marys.

So it shouldn't happen, but it does. Your friend is sick. What can you do? I'll tell you: A good plate chicken soup has cured more ills than penicillin. Chicken soup has a double-barreled action. The broth flows through the veins like plasma, bringing color to the cheeks; the *lokchen* (egg noodles) fill up the stomach so is no room left for viruses. And if you'll put in a carrot and a piece parsley, you got vitamin content, too.

For me to make a good chicken soup is easy. For my mama was hard. She would have to go to the poultry house to buy it, then she would take it to the *shechet*—the kosher slaughterer—who would kill the chicken according to ritual and for a little more money would flick the feathers off.

For me it's easy. I go to the supermarket and I ask the manager "Where by you is the kosher department?" I buy a kosher frozen chicken and I make from it a good soup.

Your friend says she isn't hungry.

"So eat anyway," you say. "From where will you get your strength?"

So she eats and you stand by so she shouldn't leave a drop. Do you think sick people know how to take care of themselves?"

Your friend says, "Ah, a *mechiah* (pleasure). I feel better already."

This is no more than you deserve after you went to so much trouble.

Of course, your friend may, God forbid, die anyway, but no one can say you didn't help her.

CHICKEN SOUP

1 young hen (4 to 5 pounds), dressed	1 whole onion
3 quarts water	1 bay leaf
1 tablespoon salt	2 carrots, peeled
	4 celery tops

Wash the chicken thoroughly and trim off excess fat. Cut the chicken in halves or quarters and place it in salted water in a deep kettle. Cover; bring to a boil. Uncover and reduce heat. Add onion, bay leaf, carrots, and celery tops. Simmer until the chicken is tender (about 3 hours). Skim when necessary. Remove the chicken to a platter and strain the soup. Chill; skim off fat that has congealed on the surface. Reheat before serving. Serves 8.

BARLEY SOUP

1 pound *flanken* (plate brisket)	2 teaspoons salt
1 marrow bone (optional)	1/2 cup pearl barley
2 quarts water	2 onions, diced
	2 carrots, diced

Cover meat and marrow bone with salted water; bring to a boil. Reduce heat and simmer for 1 hour. Skim. Wash and drain barley. Add barley and vegetables to stock. Simmer until barley is tender (about 1 1/2 hours). Pepper may be added if desired.

BARLEY AND MUSHROOM SOUP

1 ounce dried mushrooms	1 onion, diced
2 pounds soup beef (top rib or flanken)	2 carrots, diced
2 quarts water	bouquet of 2 sprigs parsley, 1 floweret of
2 teaspoons salt	dill, 1 bay leaf
1/2 cup pearl barley	pepper, to taste

Wash and soak mushrooms according to directions on package. Place meat in salted water and bring to a boil. Reduce heat and simmer about 45 minutes. Skim. Wash and drain barley. Add barley, drained mushrooms, onion, carrots, and seasonings. Simmer until meat and vegetables are tender (about 1 1/2 hours). Remove meat and bouquet. Serve hot. Serves 6.

BARLEY AND MUSHROOM SOUP

(Milchik)

1 ounce dried mushrooms	1 potato, diced
1/2 cup pearl barley	1 onion, diced
1 1/2 quarts water	1 carrot, diced
1 1/2 teaspoons salt	4 tablespoons butter
1 stalk celery, diced	1/2 cup sour cream
	pepper, to taste

Wash and soak the mushrooms according to directions on the package. Wash and drain barley. Add mushrooms, barley, and vegetables to salted water. Bring to a boil, reduce heat, and simmer until vegetables are tender (about 1 1/2 hours). Add butter. Stir in sour cream just before serving. Serves 6.

BARLEY AND SPLIT PEA SOUP

(Milchik)

1 cup green split peas	1 carrot, diced
3 tablespoons pearl barley	1 onion, diced
2 quarts water	2 tablespoons butter
2 teaspoons salt	pepper, to taste
	1 cup light cream

Cover split peas with cold water and soak overnight. Drain. Wash and drain barley. Add split peas to cold, salted water. Bring to a boil, reduce heat, and simmer until split peas are almost tender (about 1 hour). Add barley, carrot, and onion. Simmer until vegetables are tender (about 1 hour). Add butter and pepper. Stir in cream just before removing from the fire. Serve hot. Serves 8.

SPLIT PEA OR LENTIL SOUP

2 cups green split peas or lentils	2 carrots, diced
1 marrow bone	2 stalks celery, diced
	1 onion, diced

1 pound flanken
(plate brisket)
2 quarts water
2 teaspoons salt

2 frankfurters, sliced
(optional)
pepper, to taste

Cover split peas or lentils with cold water and soak over-night. Drain. Place marrow bone and cubed meat in salted water. Bring to a boil, reduce heat, and simmer for 1 hour. Skim. Add remaining ingredients (except frankfurters). Simmer until split peas or lentils are tender (about 1 1/2 hours). Remove meat and bone. Strain the soup, reserving the liquid. Rub split peas and vegetables through a sieve into the liquid. Add sliced frankfurters. Reheat and serve with pieces of meat in each serving.

Note: Mr. Alexander, the publisher, wants me to tell you how many people this will serve. This is very difficult. If you serve all of the soup at once, eight people can eat. If you serve only a part of the soup, what is left will get thick so you have to thin it out with water or soup stock. I have a friend who says when she was struggling to get her name in lights on Broadway, she lived six months on one pot of split pea soup. (I don't really believe this. I think she was a little exaggerating.) She became an expert on thinning soup. With such determination, you will not be sur-prised to hear that her name is now in lights on Broadway ... over a restaurant, not a theater.

LENTIL SOUP

[Milchik]

2 cups lentils
2 quarts water
2 teaspoons salt
2 carrots, diced

1 onion, diced
2 stalks celery, diced
2 tablespoons butter
pepper, to taste

Cover lentils with cold water and soak overnight. Drain. Add lentils and vegetables to salted water. Bring to a boil, reduce heat, and simmer until lentils are tender (about 1 1/2 hours). Strain soup, reserving the liquid. Rub vegetables through a sieve into the liquid. Add butter and seasoning. Reheat and serve. Serves 8.

SPLIT PEA SOUP

(Milchik)

Prepare as *milchike* lentil soup (above). A diced potato and a clove of garlic may be added. Remove the garlic before puréeing the vegetables.

LIMA BEAN SOUP

2 cups dried lima beans	**1 tablespoon salt**
2 onions, diced	**4 tablespoons butter or**
3 quarts water	** *schmaltz***

Cover beans with cold water and soak overnight. Drain. Add beans and onions to salted water. Bring to a rapid boil, reduce heat, and simmer until beans are tender (about 1 1/2 hours). Strain, reserving the liquid. Mash beans and onions to a pulp and return to the liquid. Add butter or *schmaltz*. Reheat and serve. Serves 10.

LIMA BEAN AND BARLEY SOUP

1 cup dried lima beans	**2 medium potatoes, diced**
1/4 cup pearl barley	**2 stalks celery, diced**
1 pound *flanken*	**2 carrots, diced**
** (plate brisket)**	**2 onions, diced**
2 1/2 quarts water	**pepper, to taste**
1 tablespoon salt	

Cover beans with cold water and soak overnight. Drain. Wash and drain barley. Place meat in salted water. Bring to a rapid boil, reduce heat, and simmer 45 minutes. Add beans, barley, and vegetables. Bring to a boil, reduce heat, and simmer about 1 1/2 hours or until beans are tender. Skim when necessary while cooking. Serve hot. Serves 6.

CREAM OF SPINACH SOUP

4 tablespoons butter
4 tablespoons flour
1 quart milk
1/4 cup minced onions

1 cup cooked and
  puréed spinach
1 teaspoon salt
pepper, to taste

Melt butter in a 2–quart saucepan. Add flour, stirring until smooth. Gradually add milk, stirring constantly. Add spinach, onions, and seasonings. Simmer 10 minutes. Serves 4.

COLD CHERRY SOUP

1 32 ounce can tart red
  cherries, pitted
1 quart water
1/4 cup sugar

1 teaspoon salt
1 stick cinnamon
1 tablespoon cornstarch
1/2 cup sour cream

Boil cherries, water, sugar, salt, and cinnamon for 10 minutes. Make a thin paste of cornstarch and 1/4 cup cold water. Slowly add the paste to the boiling cherries. Continue to boil for 5 minutes. Remove from heat. Remove cinnamon and chill thoroughly. Stir in sour cream just before serving. Serves 6.

CHERRY AND WINE SOUP

1 quart fresh sweet black
  cherries (do not pit)
2 cups water
1/4 cup sugar (about)
1/2 lemon, thinly sliced

1 stick cinnamon
1 tablespoon cornstarch
1/4 cup cold water
1 cup claret
whipped cream

Bring to a boil cherries, water, sugar, lemon, and cinnamon. Reduce heat and simmer 15 minutes. Make a smooth paste of cornstarch and water. Slowly add to the soup. Cook 10 minutes, stirring constantly. Remove from the heat. Remove cinnamon. Add wine slowly, stirring constantly. Chill thoroughly. Garnish with whipped cream. Serves 6.

RUSSEL

(Sour beet juice)

beets   **boiled water**

Remove greens and tops of beets and wash them thoroughly, scrubbing with a stiff vegetable brush. Quarter beets and place them in an earthenware crock with a tight cover. Cover beets with boiled water that has been cooled to lukewarm. There must be at least 2 inches of water above the beets. Cover and let stand in a warm place about 4 weeks.

Note: The sour beet juice *(russel)* is used for borsch.

RUSSEL BORSCH

2 pounds plate brisket
1 onion
3 bay leaves
5 cups cold water
2 teaspoons salt

4 cups russel (sour beet juice; see above)
sugar and pepper, to taste
3 eggs, beaten
hot boiled potatoes garnish (see below)

Cook meat, onion, and bay leaves in salted water at a slow boil until the meat is tender. Add russel, sugar, and pepper. Bring to a boil, reduce heat, and simmer for 15 minutes. Slowly pour borsch into the beaten eggs, stirring constantly. Place a hot boiled potato and pieces of meat in each serving of soup, or garnish with hard-boiled egg slices, parsley, or bits of matzos. Serves 6.

Note: Russel borsch is traditionally served during Passover week.

RUSSEL BORSCH

(Milchik)

6 cups russel (sour beet juice)
2 cups shredded russel beets

1 tablespoon sugar (about)
6 tablespoons sour cream
hot boiled potatoes

1 onion, diced   garnish (see below)
1 1/2 teaspoons salt

Bring russel, beets, onion, salt, and sugar to a boil. Reduce
heat and simmer for 15 minutes. Remove from heat and
chill thoroughly. Just before serving, stir into each portion
1 tablespoon sour cream and place a hot boiled potato in it.
Garnish with thinly sliced cucumbers, hard boiled egg
slices, or minced parsley. Serves 6.

FLAISHIK BORSCH

2 bunches (about 10)   2 tablespoons sugar
    small beets   (about)*
2 onions, sliced   2 teaspoons salt
2 pounds plate brisket   pepper, to taste
2 quarts water   matzos for garnish
juice of 2 lemons

Peel and slice or dice beets. Place beets, onions, and meat in
a deep kettle. Add water and bring to a boil. Reduce heat
and simmer until the meat is tender. Add lemon juice,
sugar, salt, and pepper. Simmer 10 minutes longer. Serve
hot with with pieces of meat in each serving and a garnish
of crumbled matzos. Serves 8.

Note: It is impossible to give exact measurements for sugar.
Some like it sour, some like it sweet. Just keep tasting and
adjusting lemon juice and sugar until it is the way you like it.

CABBAGE BORSCH

2 pounds plate brisket   1/2 cup seedless raisins
1 marrow bone   juice of 2 lemons
1 onion, diced   1/4 cup brown sugar
2 cups canned tomatoes   2 teaspoons salt
1 small head cabbage,   pepper, to taste
    shredded

Bring meat, marrow bone, and 1 1/2 quarts water to a rapid
boil. Skim. Add onion and tomatoes. Bring to a boil again,

reduce heat, and simmer until meat is tender (about 2 hours). Sprinkle the shredded cabbage with a handful of salt and let it stand while the soup is cooking. Drench with hot water and drain. Add cabbage and raisins to borsch. Cover and simmer until the cabbage is tender (about 30 minutes). Add lemon juice, sugar, salt, and pepper. Simmer 10 minutes longer. Serve hot with pieces of meat in each serving. Serves 8.

COLD BORSCH

2 bunches (about 10) small beets, peeled and diced	1 tablespoon sugar (about)
2 quarts water	3 eggs
2 teaspoons salt	1 cup sour cream
juice of 1 lemon	hot boiled potatoes
	garnish (see below)

Cook beets in water, uncovered, until tender. Add salt, lemon juice, and sugar. (The amount of sugar will vary according to taste.) Simmer for 10 minutes. Beat eggs thoroughly in a large mixing bowl. Add hot beet liquid to the eggs very slowly, stirring constantly. Chill thoroughly. When ready to serve, stir 1 tablespoon sour cream into each serving. A hot boiled potato may be added to each serving, or the borsch may be garnished with thinly sliced cucumber or minced parsley. Serves 8.

ISRAELI BORSCH

2 bunches (about 10) small beets	2 teaspoons salt
2 carrots	juice of 1 lemon
1 onion, grated	1 tablespoon sugar (about)
2 quarts water	sour cream

Peel and shred beets and carrots. Add the onion and cook, uncovered, in salted water until tender (about 25 minutes). Add lemon juice and sugar. Simmer 10 minutes longer.

Remove from heat and chill thoroughly. Garnish with 1 tablespoon sour cream for each serving. Serves 8.

SCHAV

1 pound *schav* (sorrel grass) or 1 pound spinach	juice of 2 lemons
	2 tablespoons sugar (about)
	1 cup sour cream
1 quart water	hot boiled potatoes
1 teaspoon salt	garnish (see below)

Wash *schav* or spinach in several waters. Drain. Remove stems and chop or cut up the leaves. Place in salted water and bring to a boil. Reduce heat and simmer for 10 minutes. Add lemon juice and sugar. Simmer 10 minutes longer. Remove from heat and chill thoroughly. Stir sour cream into *schav* just before serving. A hot boiled potato may be served with *schav*. Garnish with sliced tops of green onions or sliced hard-boiled eggs. Serves 6.

GOURMET'S SCHAV

1 pound *schav* or spinach	2 quarts water
	juice of 2 lemons
2 medium-sized potatoes, diced	2 teaspoons salt
	1/4 teaspoon pepper
4 green onions, sliced	8 eggs
2 flowerets of dill	3 cups cold water

Wash greens in several waters. Remove stems and cut leaves in half. Place greens, potatoes, green onions, and dill in water and bring to a boil. Reduce heat and simmer until potatoes are done (about 20 minutes). Add lemon juice, salt, and pepper. Simmer 10 minutes longer. Remove dill. Beat eggs with 3 cups cold water until light. Very slowly pour 4 cups of the soup stock into the egg mixture, stirring constantly to prevent curdling. Remove soup from heat and add egg mixture to it. Chill thoroughly. Serves 8 to 10.

POTATO SOUP

(Milchik)

3 cups diced potatoes	3 sprigs parsley
1 cup diced onions	1 cup sour cream
2 stalks celery, diced	2 tablespoons minced
1 quart water	parsley for garnish
2 teaspoons salt	paprika
1 quart milk	1/8 pound butter (or more)

Cook potatoes, onions, and celery in salted water until tender (about 30 minutes). Remove from heat. Mash vegetables with a potato masher. Add milk, butter, and parsley. Return to heat and simmer gently for about 15 minutes (do not allow to boil). Remove parsley. Stir in sour cream and allow the soup to remain over low heat just long enough to heat the cream. Garnish with minced parsley and paprika. Serves 8.

♥ 4 ♥

OODLES OF NOODLES OR MY WAR WITH LOKCHEN

Nowadays, people aren't making *lokchen* any more. This is to me not a surprise. When I tell you how to make *lokchen* (noodles), so you won't be surprised they are not making it, either.

My mama could make *lokchen* as thin as a thread, so one day I asked her, "Mama, how do you make *lokchen*?"

"Why do you want to make *lokchen*?"

"Why shouldn't I want?"

"Because," said Mama, "the way you will make *lokchen* you should better buy at the store."

"So what's so hard to make *lokchen*?"

"Who says it's hard? You put in a little flour, a little egg, and you got *lokchen*."

"How much?"

"How much you want. You want a lot, you put in a lot. You don't want so much, you don't put in so much."

From this I'm not learning to make *lokchen*. I try again.

"Mama, you make the *lokchen*. I'll watch. But everything must be measured."

So good already. No. While she is measuring the flour, the phone rings. When I come back from the phone, she tells me, "I put in two and a half cups flour, but I see already it's too much."

I empty the flour from the bowl.

"What are you doing with my flour?" screams Mama.

"It's too much you say. So I'm putting back we should measure again."

"But I took out already a little with the hand. Now is right."

So what shall I tell you? Eventually, I'm getting the measurements. We're making the dough, and hard it really isn't. But it's not over yet the lesson. The trouble comes when you stretch the dough.

Mama could make a perfect round of noodle dough so big it hung over the kitchen table. So how did she do it? With a broomstick she did it. Rolling pins were only for those who cooked from books. With 2 1/2 feet of broom handle, Mama would roll the dough, turning it after each roll to keep its roundness.

(When I first started my war with *lokchen*, before I came out a winner, I found it easier to turn the cook than to turn the thin noodle sheet. I worked my way slowly around the table. This served two purposes: while the dough got thinner, I got thinner.)

As Mama's noodle dough became thin, she would put the palm of her left hand on the part nearest her. The opposite end she would wrap around the broomstick two or three times, then with the palm of her right hand on the center of the noodle–wrapped stick, she would roll it away from her with short, quick motions, stretching with each roll until the noodle banner was unfurled.

When she had gone as far as she could with her home-made rolling pin, she would gently lift the edges of the dough and stretch it more. When the noodle sheet positively and absolutely couldn't stand another strain, she would leave it to dry for about half an hour ... it shouldn't get too dry. She would then roll it like a jelly roll. Then, with the fingertips of her left hand placed 1/16 inch from the edge, she would start slicing. You could never mistake the noodle-making sound of the knife hitting the board. Chop-chop-chop, a steady rhythm, never losing a beat or a fingertip.

The way I look at it, a cook should attack a noodle dough like she was the aggressor in a cold war. She should pull at it, she should tug at it, she should nag at it until just before she or it reaches the breaking point. Believe me, this is not an unequal battle. Either side may win. The object is that the cold war should end with friendly relations, but the *lokchen* should know who is boss.

LOKCHEN

(Noodles)

1/2 teaspoon salt
2 scant cups unsifted flour

2 eggs, slightly beaten

Add salt to eggs. Add eggs to flour. Mix thoroughly with the hand until the dough leaves the sides of the bowl. (This should make a fairly stiff dough; when thoroughly mixed, it will not cling to the hands.) Knead until the dough is smooth and elastic. Roll out on a lightly floured white cloth that has been stretched over the kitchen table. Roll and stretch to paper thinness. Let stand until the noodle sheet feels dry (about 30 minutes). The exact time cannot be given, since it will vary according to temperature, humidity, and thickness of dough. It should be dry enough to roll like a jelly roll without sticking together. If it dries too long it becomes brittle and is impossible to roll up. Roll up loosely; cut crosswise in very thin strips. (See "Oodles of Noodles" for directions.) Toss lightly to separate the strands. Allow to dry completely (at least an hour) before storing in a jar or plastic bag. When ready to use, drop in rapidly boiling, salted water or soup and cook for 10 minutes.

PLAETSCHEN

(Noodle Squares)

Prepare noodle dough as in preceding recipe. Roll out as for noodles and allow to dry about 30 minutes. Cut into 1/2-inch strips. Stack strips and cut into 1/2–inch squares. Dry and store. Cook in boiling, salted water or in soup for 15 minutes.

OOPHLAIFERS OR FINGERHUETCHEN

(Thimble Noodles)

Prepare noodle dough (see recipe on page 25) and roll out as for noodles. Let stand about 15 minutes. Fold dough over once. With a floured thimble, cut through both thicknesses. Drop into deep hot fat and fry until lightly browned (about 1 minute). *Fingerhuetchen* will puff up to form tiny balls. Drain on a paper towel. Serve in clear chicken soup.

MANDLEN

2 cups sifted flour　　**2 tablespoons salad oil**
3 eggs, slightly beaten　　**1 teaspoon salt**

Mix all ingredients with a pastry blender.* This should make a dough firm enough to roll with your hands. Divide the dough into four parts. Roll each part between the floured palms of your hands to form pencil-like strips. Cut strips into 1/2-inch pieces. Bake on a well-oiled shallow pan at 375 degrees until golden brown (about 20 minutes). Shake pan occasionally so that *mandlen* will brown evenly. Heat in soup a few minutes before serving.

*Your grandmother didn't use a pastry blender, but then, she didn't have to run to answer the phone just when she started mixing the dough.

FARFEL

1/4 teaspoon salt   **1 1/2 cups unsifted flour**
1 egg, slightly beaten

Add salt to beaten egg. Add egg to flour. Mix with the fingers to form a very stiff ball of dough. Let stand until hard enough to grate (about 1 hour). Grate on the large side of a grater. Toss to separate, and spread thinly on a platter. Dry completely before storing in a jar or plastic bag. When ready to use, drop in boiling salted water or soup. Cook 10 minutes.

EINLAUF

1 egg   **pinch of salt**
4 tablespoons cold water   **3 tablespoons flour**

Beat egg with water. Add salt. Add egg mixture to flour, stirring until smooth. Slowly drop a thin stream of the mixture from the end of a spoon into boiling soup. Cook 5 minutes.

SOUP CAKES

2 tablespoons melted   **1 teaspoon baking**
     ***schmaltz* or shortening**   **powder**
2 eggs, slightly beaten   **3/4 cup cold water**
1 1/2 cups sifted flour

Stir melted *schmaltz* or shortening into the eggs. Sift flour with baking powder. Add to eggs. Add water and stir until smooth. Fill lightly greased toy muffin tins two thirds full, or large muffin tins half full. Bake at 400 degrees until lightly browned (about 30 minutes). Serve in hot, clear chicken soup. Makes 12 large cakes or 24 small ones.

LOKCHEN KUGEL

1/2 pound noodles, cooked	1/4 cup *grebenes* (cracklings; see p. 46)
1/2 cup melted *schmaltz*	3 eggs, well beaten

Combine all ingredients. Place in a well–greased 1 1/2 quart casserole. Bake at 375 degrees until top is lightly browned (about 1 hour). Serve as a soup accompaniment or in place of potatoes with a meat dinner. Serves 6.

PIROSHKI

1 1/2 cups sifted flour	1/2 cup shortening
1/2 teaspoon salt	1/4 cup cold water (or less)
1/4 teaspoon baking powder	

Sift together dry ingredients. Cut in shortening until pieces are the size of a pea, adding just enough water to hold the mixture together. Roll out as a pie crust on a floured board. Cut into 3 inch squares or rounds, and place a teaspoon of filling in the center of each. Fold squares crosswise to form triangles, or form rounds into half-moons. Press edges together firmly with the floured tines of a fork. Place on a baking tin generously greased with *schmaltz* or shortening. Bake at 400 degrees until golden brown (about 20 minutes). Serve as a soup accompaniment. Makes about 30.

PIROSHKI FILLINGS

Lung–Chicken

1 small onion, chopped	1 cup cooked chicken
2 tablespoons *schmaltz* or shortening	2 broiled chicken livers
1 pound small beef lungs, boiled	1 egg, beaten
	salt and pepper, to taste

Saute onion in *schmaltz* or shortening. Chop or grind together lungs, chicken, and livers. Add onion and the *schmaltz* in which it has been sauteed to the meat. Add egg and seasonings. Blend well.

Meat

1 onion, minced	1 pound ground beef or
2 tablespoons *schmaltz*	1 pound ground
salt and pepper, to taste	leftover meat

Saute onion in *schmaltz*. Add meat and seasonings. Saute until meat is browned.

Kasha (Buckwheat Groats)

1 onion, minced	2 cups cooked kasha (see
2 tablespoons *schmaltz*	page 94)
salt and pepper, to taste	

Saute onion in *schmaltz*. Add onion, the *schmaltz* in which it has been sauteed, and seasonings to the prepared kasha.

Note: Kasha may be moistened with chicken or meat gravy instead of *schmaltz*. There are many variations on *piroshki* fillings. You can experiment on your own. Go ahead! Enjoy!

KREPLECH

Prepare noodle dough (see page 25). Roll out as for noodles, but do not dry. Cut into 3 inch squares. Place 1 teaspoon filling in the center of each square. Fold crosswise to form triangles. Press the edges together firmly with the floured tines of a fork. Drop in boiling, salted water or soup. Cook 15 minutes. They will rise to the top when done.

Note: Kreplech may be served in soup or may be cooked in boiling water, then drained and fried in hot fat until brown on both sides. Cheese *kreplech* may be cooked in boiling water, then drained and baked in a buttered pan at 375 degrees until brown (about 40 minutes). Makes about 30.

KREPLECH FILLINGS

Chicken Liver

2 cups broiled chicken
     livers
2 hard-boiled eggs
1 small onion

salt and pepper, to taste
1 tablespoon *schmaltz*
     (about)

Chop livers, eggs, and onion together finely. Season to taste. Add just enough *schmaltz* to hold the ingredients together.

Chicken

2 cups cooked chicken,
     ground
1 tablespoon minced
     onion

1 egg
salt and pepper, to taste
1 tablespoon minced
     parsley

Combine all ingredients.

Meat

2 cups cooked meat,
     ground, or 2 cups
     ground beef, browned

1 egg
1 tablespoon minced onion
salt and pepper, to taste

Combine all ingredients. If fresh meat is used, brown it with onion in hot *schmaltz*. Season and mix with the egg.

Cheese

2 cups dry cottage cheese
2 tablespoons fine bread
     crumbs

2 tablespoons sour cream
salt and pepper, to taste
1 egg

Combine all ingredients.

KNISHES

5 cups unsifted flour
1/4 cup sugar
pinch of salt

3/4 cup salad oil
3 eggs, beaten
1 cup lukewarm water

Sift together dry ingredients. Make a well in the center and add oil, eggs, and water. Mix thoroughly. Dust a bowl with flour; invert for a moment to remove excess flour. Place dough in the floured bowl and cover with a tea towel. Let stand for 15 minutes. Knead well on a lightly floured white cloth stretched over the kitchen table.

Divide the dough into four parts. Work with one part, keeping the remainder in the covered bowl. Fill one part of the dough before rolling out the next; the sheets of dough will become too dry if allowed to stand. Assembly line techniques are for the factory, not the kitchen.

Roll and stretch dough into a round sheet about 20 inches in diameter. Brush the sheet with salad oil or melted butter. Starting 1 1/2 inches from edge nearest you, place a line of filling (see recipes on following pages. Double the amounts given there.) 1 1/2 inches wide and 1 inch thick across the width of the sheet of dough. Lift the flap nearest you to cover the filling, then roll the filled dough twice. Cut this part away from the remainder of the sheet of dough.

Repeat the process until all the dough has been used. Brush the tops of the filled rolls with oil or melted butter. Slice at 1 1/2 inch intervals. Upend each slice, cut side down, on a liberally oiled baking tin. Press down on each slice with the palm of the hand so that it is flattened and rounded. Bake at 350 degrees until lightly browned (about 1 hour). Some cooks prefer to turn the knishes when they are brown on the bottom. Serve piping hot as a soup accompaniment. Makes about 60.

Note: Sixty knishes is a lot of knishes, but if you are going to the trouble to make knishes so you might as well have a lot of knishes. You can put them in your freezer. They are even more delicious after being frozen. Reheat in an ungreased baking tin for 20 minutes at 350 degrees.

BAKING POWDER KNISHES

2 cups flour
1 teaspoon baking
　　powder

1/2 teaspoon salt
2 tablespoons salad oil
2 eggs, beaten

Sift together dry ingredients. Add oil and eggs. Blend thoroughly. If necessary, add a little water to hold the dough together. Follow directions in preceding recipe for rolling, stretching, filling, and baking. Serve as a soup accompaniment. Makes 30.

KNISH FILLINGS

(for 30 knishes)

Cheese

3 to 5* large onions,
　　browned
1/4 pound butter
2 1/2 pounds dry cottage
　　cheese

3 tablespoons sour cream
2 tablespoons sugar
1/4 teaspoon salt
3 eggs

Saute onions in butter until golden. Blend together all ingredients.

*How many onions depends only upon how well you like them.

Potato

3 onions, chopped
1/2 cup *schmaltz* or
　　1/4 pound butter

1 egg
salt and pepper, to taste
2 cups mashed potatoes

Saute onions in *schmaltz* or butter until golden. Blend together all ingredients.

Meat

1 onion, chopped
1 tablespoon *schmaltz*
1 cup cooked beef
1 cup boiled lung
1 egg

1 cup cooked kasha,
　　cooked rice, or
　　mashed potatoes
salt and pepper, to taste

Saute onion in *schmaltz* until golden. Grind beef and lung together. Combine all ingredients.

Kasha

2 onions, minced
2 tablespoons *schmaltz*
2 cups cooked kasha
   (see page 94)

salt and pepper, to taste
chicken or meat gravy

Saute onions in *schmaltz* until golden. Combine with kasha Add seasonings and just enough gravy to moisten.

Chicken

2 cups ground cooked
   chicken
1/2 cup mashed potatoes

salt and pepper, to taste
2 tablespoons chicken
   gravy

Combine all ingredients.

Note: Knish fillings may be made of all kinds of leftover meat or poultry combined with mashed potatoes, cooked rice, or kasha. Try a filling of rice, egg, cinnamon–sugar mix, and raisins. Anything too good to throw away may be put in knishes.

CHEESE KNISHES

Dough

2 cups sifted flour
1 teaspoon baking
   powder
1/4 teaspoon salt

1 egg, beaten
1/2 cup sour cream
1 tablespoon melted
   butter

Sift together dry ingredients. Add egg, sour cream, and butter. Blend thoroughly and knead well. Follow directions on page 31 for rolling, stretching, and filling dough. Place on a shallow baking tin that has been liberally greased with melted butter. Bake at 350 degrees until lightly browned (about 1 hour), basting occasionally with melted butter. Makes about 30.

Filling

1/2 pound dry cottage
  cheese
2 tablespoons sour cream
2 tablespoons bread
  crumbs

1 tablespoon sugar
1 tablespoon melted
  butter
2 eggs, beaten
1/4 cup seedless raisins

Combine all ingredients.

HALKES

[Dumplings]

2 cups grated raw
  potatoes*
1 teaspoon grated onion
1 egg
2/3 cup flour (about)

1 1/2 teaspoons salt
pepper, to taste
3 tablespoons bread
  crumbs

Combine all ingredients into a batter that should be firm enough to form into balls the size of a walnut. If necessary, add more flour. Drop the balls into rapidly boiling salted water. Cook about 20 minutes. The *halkes* will rise to the top when done. Serve in clear soup or with meat or chicken gravy. Serves 6.

*Measure the potatoes after draining well.

EGG KICHLECH

2 scant cups sifted flour
3 teaspoons baking
  powder
1/2 teaspoon salt

3 eggs, beaten
1 teaspoon salad oil
granulated sugar

Sift together the flour, baking powder, and salt. Add oil to beaten eggs. Add egg mixture to flour mixture. Mix thoroughly. Knead for about 5 minutes. Roll out on a lightly floured board to 1/4 inch thickness. Sprinkle with sugar. Cut into rectangles 2 by 4 inches. Place on lightly floured baking tins. Bake at 400 degrees for 10 minutes. Makes about 24.

DEEP–FRIED EGG KICHLECH

2 eggs
2 teaspoons lemon juice
1 teaspoon vanilla
1 tablespoon sugar

1/2 teaspoon salt
1 1/2 cups flour (about)
powdered sugar

Beat eggs. Add lemon juice, vanilla, sugar, and salt. Add enough flour to be able to roll out the dough. Knead lightly. Roll out to 1/8 inch thickness and cut into diamond shapes 4 inches long. Fry quickly in deep fat until golden brown. Drain on brown paper and sprinkle with powdered sugar. Serve as a soup accompaniment. Makes about 24.

♥ 5 ♥

MILCHIKS IS MILCHIKS

*M*ilchiks is *milchiks* and *flaishiks* is *flaishiks* and on the table of an orthodox Jew the two should never meet. The saying I'm taking from Mr. Kipling, also a writer, except I'm changing a little because Mr. Kipling is saying "East is East and West is West," but if he should ask me, I would tell him that East will meet West before *milchiks* will meet *flaishiks*. This is the law. Dairy foods will never be eaten with meat because it is written that a kid should not be stewed in the milk of its mother.

From all this you can see that mixing *milchiks* and *flaishiks* is not a laughing matter. So you will understand just how serious it is, I'll tell to you a story about a poor *schlimazel* (unfortunate) who lived in a village in Poland. "Lived," I say, but who could call it living? The way he lived you wouldn't wish it on your worst enemy. The only thing he had a lot of was children and these he couldn't feed. Everything he put his hand to failed. If he sold bread, people stopped eating. If he sold shrouds, it was his misfortune, people stopped dying. What shall I tell you? His poor children were crying from hunger.

So how long can you listen when children cry? Finally, the poor *schlimazel* couldn't stand it any more. He made up his mind he would steal, he would rob, he would murder ... anything to feed his children. "God will forgive me for this," thought the *schlimazel*.

So he took from the kitchen a knife and went out on the highway he should find for himself a rich victim. For the first time in his life, he was lucky. Right away comes walking by a rich victim.

Our *schlimazel* was strong like an ox, so one-two-three he knocks down the rich victim and is ready to stick in him the knife when he sees his mistake.

"So go already in good health," he cries, letting go of the rich man. "It is your good fortune that by mistake I took with me my *milchike* knife."*

This only goes to show that a *schlimazel* is usually also a *schlimiehl* (one who creates his own misfortune).

From this you are not learning how to cook, so turn over the page and I'll give you recipes how to cook *milchiks*, but don't mix up the knives.

*Adapted from a story in *A Treasury of Jewish Folklore,* by Nathan Ausubela, by courtesy of Crown Publishers, Inc.

CHEESE NOODLES

1/2 pound broad noodles   1 cup cottage cheese
1 tablespoon butter

Cook noodles in rapidly boiling salted water until tender (about 10 minutes). Drain, rinse with hot water, and drain again. Combine with cottage cheese and butter. Serve immediately. Serves 6.

CHEESE NOODLE RING

3 ounces cream cheese
1/2 cup cottage cheese, drained
2 eggs

1/2 teaspoon salt
3 cups boiled noodles
cracker crumbs
butter

Work cream cheese and drained cottage cheese together with a fork until well blended. Beat eggs into the cheese mixture. Add salt and noodles. Mix well.

Place in a liberally buttered ring mold. Cover with cracker crumbs and dot with butter. Bake at 375 degrees until the top is lightly browned (about 1 hour). Unmold and serve hot or cold. Serves 6.

APPLE NOODLES

4 tablespoons sugar
1/2 teaspoon cinnamon
1/4 teaspoon ground cloves

4 cups cooked broad noodles
butter
4 cups sliced tart apples

Combine sugar, cinnamon, and cloves. Using a 2 quart casserole, butter it well and in it place alternate layers of noodles, dotted with butter, and apples sprinkled with the sugar-spice mix. Use noodles for the bottom and top layers.

Bake covered at 375 degrees until the apples are tender (about 45 minutes). Uncover and bake 15 minutes longer. Serves 6.

CARROT PUDDING

1 pound carrots	pinch of salt
1 tablespoon butter	1 teaspoon cinnamon
4 tablespoons sugar	1/4 teaspoon nutmeg
4 eggs, separated	3 tablespoons butter
grated peel of 1 lemon	cinnamon-sugar mix (1
3 tablespoons flour	teaspoon cinnamon
1 teaspoon baking powder	to 1/4 cup sugar)

Peel and boil carrots until tender (about 20 minutes). Grate. Cream together 1 tablespoon butter and the sugar. Beat egg yolks until light and add to butter–sugar mixture. Add lemon peel. Sift together flour, baking powder, salt, cinnamon, and nutmeg. Stir into the egg mixture. Add the grated carrots. Fold in stiffly beaten egg whites.

Melt 3 tablespoons butter in a 1 quart casserole. Pour in the pudding batter. Bake at 350 degrees for 1 hour. Remove from oven and sprinkle with cinnamon–sugar mix.

Place under broiler for about 5 minutes or until cinnamon–sugar mix browns. Serve as a side dish with dairy dishes. Serves 6.

NOODLES AND PRUNES

2 cups stewed prunes	3 cups cooked noodles
1/4 teaspoon cinnamon	butter
mixed with 1 table-	bread crumbs
spoon sugar	1 cup prune juice

Remove prune pits and sprinkle prunes with cinnamon–sugar mix. Using a 1 1/2 quart casserole, butter it well and in it place alternate layers of noodles, dotted with butter, and prunes.

Use noodles for the bottom and top layers. Pour prune juice over all. Cover with bread crumbs and dot with butter. Bake at 375 degrees until the crumbs are browned (about 1 hour). Serves 6.

POPPY SEED NOODLES

1/2 pound broad noodles
1/2 cup salted almonds,
chopped
1/8 pound butter

1 teaspoon lemon juice
2 tablespoons poppy seed
pepper (optional)

Cook noodles in boiling salted water until tender (about 10 minutes). While the noodles are cooking, heat almonds in butter but do not brown. Add lemon juice and poppy seed to almonds. Drain the noodles, place in a serving bowl, and stir into them the almond–poppy seed mixture. Serve immediately. Serves 6.

LOKCHEN KUGEL

2 eggs, beaten
3 tablespoons sugar
1/4 teaspoon cinnamon
1/2 pound noodles*,
cooked and drained

4 tablespoons butter,
melted
pinch of salt
1/2 cup seedless raisins,
chopped

Combine eggs, sugar, cinnamon, and salt. Add to the noodles. Add melted butter and raisins. Mix thoroughly. Place in a liberally buttered 1 1/2 quart casserole and bake at 400 degrees until lightly browned (about 45 minutes). Serves 6.

Note: Either broad or fine noodles may be used.

LOKCHEN KUGEL WITH APPLES

2 eggs, beaten
3 tablespoons sugar
1/4 teaspoon cinnamon
pinch of salt
1/2 pound noodles*,
cooked and drained

1 cup shredded tart
apples
1/4 cup raisins
1/4 cup chopped nuts
4 tablespoons melted
butter⁺

Combine eggs, sugar, cinnamon, and salt. Add to the noodles. Add apples, raisins, nuts, and melted butter. Mix thoroughly. Place in a well-greased 1 1/2 quart casserole. Bake at 400 degrees until brown on top (about 1 hour). Serves 6.

*Either broad or fine noodles may be used.

⁺*Schmaltz* may be substituted for butter if the *kugel* is to be served with meat.

LOKCHEN KUGEL WITH APRICOTS

1/2 pound noodles	**1/4 teaspoon salt**
1/2 pound dried apricots, diced	**dash of nutmeg**
	1/4 teaspoon cinnamon
2 eggs, beaten	**2 tablespoons melted**
1/3 cup sugar	**butter⁺**

Cook noodles in rapidly boiling salted water until tender (about 10 minutes). Soak apricots in hot water for 5 minutes. Drain. Combine eggs, sugar, salt, nutmeg, cinnamon, and drained noodles. Stir in drained apricots and melted butter. Bake in a greased 1 1/2 quart casserole at 375 degrees until lightly browned (about 45 minutes). Serves 6.

⁺*Schmaltz* may be used if the kugel is to be served with meat.

RICE KUGEL

1 cup rice	**grated peel of 1 lemon**
4 tablespoons butter	**3 eggs**
1 scant cup confectioners sugar	**1/4 cup chopped nuts**
	1/2 cup seedless raisins
1/2 teaspoon cinnamon	

Cook rice until tender, following directions on package. Drain and set aside. Cream together butter and sugar. Add cinnamon and lemon peel. Add eggs one at a time, beating well after each addition. Stir in nuts and raisins, then add the cooked rice. Bake in a well-greased 1 quart casserole at 350 degrees for 1 hour. Serve hot or cold. Serves 6.

POTATO KUGEL

1 large onion, minced
2 eggs, beaten
1/8 pound butter*
2 cups grated raw potatoes
   (measure after drain-
   ing well)

1/2 teaspoon baking
   powder
1/2 cup flour
1 1/2 teaspoons salt
pepper, to taste

Saute onion in butter until lightly browned. Add eggs to potatoes. Sift together dry ingredients and add to potato mixture. Stir in the onions and butter in which they have been sauteed. Pour into a well–greased 1 quart casserole. Bake at 350 degrees until the edges are crisp (about 1 hour). Serves 6.

*Note: Schmaltz may be substituted for butter when kugel is to be served with meat dishes.

BAKED CHEESE KREPLECH

3 1/2 cups sifted flour
3 teaspoons baking
   powder
1 teaspoon salt

1 cup sour cream
2 eggs, well beaten
1/2 cup melted butter

Sift together dry ingredients. Mix sour cream with eggs and butter. Stir in dry ingredients and knead for about 2 minutes. Roll out on a lightly floured board to 1/4 inch thickness. Cut into 4 inch squares. Place a tablespoon of cheese filling on each square. Fold over crosswise to form a triangle; pinch the edges together firmly. Place in a liberally buttered baking dish. Bake at 375 degrees until lightly browned (about 40 minutes). Serves 6.

FILLING

3 ounces cream cheese
1/2 pound dry cottage
   cheese
1 teaspoon sugar

pinch of salt
1 egg
2 tablespoons melted
   butter*

Blend together cream cheese, cottage cheese, sugar, and salt, using a fork. Beat in the egg and add melted butter. Mix well.

SALTINOSSES

Prepare noodle dough (see page 25). Roll out as for noodles, but do not dry. Cut into oblongs 3 by 6 inches. In the center of each oblong place 1 tablespoon cottage cheese filling (see page 46; add a liberal amount of pepper).

Raise the bottom flap of dough to cover the filling, and cover both with the top flap of dough. Pinch the edges together firmly. Drop into rapidly boiling salted water.

Cook until they rise to the top of the water. Remove and drain. Place in a well–buttered baking dish. Cover with sour cream, salt, and pepper. Bake at 375 degrees until the tops are lightly browned (about 45 minutes). Serves 6 to 8.

VARENIKES

Prepare noodle dough (see page 25). Roll very thin but do not dry. Cut in 3 inch rounds. Place 1 teaspoon filling in the center of each round. Fold over into half-moons and pinch edges together firmly.

Drop into rapidly boiling salted water. Cook until they rise to the top. Remove and drain. Place in a buttered baking dish. Baste with melted butter. Bake at 375 degrees until lightly browned (about 40 minutes). Serve with sour cream. Serves 6 to 8.

FILLINGS FOR VARENIKES

Fruit

2 cups blueberries or pitted cherries

sugar, to taste
1 tablespoon cornstarch

Stew fruit with sugar. Make a paste of cornstarch and 1/4 cup lukewarm fruit juice. Add to the fruit and cook until thickened. Cool.

Cheese

Follow recipe for cheese filling for knishes (see page 32), using one third the amounts.

KASHA VARNITCHKES

2 cups cooked kasha   **1 cup cooked noodle**
** (see page 94)**   ** squares**
4 tablespoons melted
** butter**

Prepare kasha and add cooked noodles. Place in a greased 1 quart casserole. Pour melted butter over all. Bake at 350 degrees for 20 minutes. Serves 4 to 6.

BLINTZES

1 cup flour   **1 cup water or milk**
1/2 teaspoon salt   **butter**
4 eggs

Sift together flour and salt. Beat eggs; add liquid; beat again. Gradually add flour to eggs, stirring constantly to make a thin, smooth batter. Lightly grease a 6 inch skillet with butter. Place skillet over moderately high heat.

Fill a cup with batter. Pour about 1/2 cupful batter into the skillet. As soon as the batter sticks to the skillet, pour the excess back into the cup. Fry until the blintze begins to "blister" and the edges curl away from the skillet; the top of the blintze may still be slightly moist. Turn out, fried side up, by inverting the skillet over a wooden board. It may be necessary to tap the edge of the skillet against the board.

The skillet should be greased at about every third blintze. When blintzes are all fried, fill with any of the following fillings.

Place 1 tablespoon filling in the center of each blintze (on the browned side). Raise the bottom flap of dough to cover the filling, then overlap with top flap of dough. Tuck both sides under so that they almost meet at the back center. Fry in a liberal amount of butter until lightly browned on both sides. Serve hot with apple sauce or sour cream. Serves 6.

BLINTZE FILLINGS

Cheese

1 pound dry cottage cheese
1 egg yolk
1 tablespoon sugar

1 tablespoon melted butter
pinch of salt

Combine all ingredients.

Blueberry

2 tablespoons sugar
2 cups blueberries

2 tablespoons flour

Sprinkle blueberries with sugar and flour.

Apple

2 cups chopped apples
2 egg whites

1/2 cup chopped nuts
sugar and cinnamon, to taste

Combine all ingredients.

Meat

For meat filling, see *kreplech* or *piroshki* fillings (pages 28 and 30).

♥ 6 ♥

Put Some Schmaltz in it

W hen you are hearing the expression: "Put some *schmaltz* in it," so you don't know what they are talking about. Is it cooking, is it music, is it acting?

I am reading lately about a school in New York called Actors Studio and it's here where actors are learning to act. You think maybe they are learning to act like human beings? No. Here the teacher is telling them to act like a telephone, to make like a subway which it is the rush hour, to make like a frying pan. In other words, make like an inanimate object.

Now, the actor who is making like a frying pan, if he is just making like a plain frying pan, is putting on a cold performance and this is not good. If he is a good actor, he'll put some *schmaltz* in it.

When you put *schmaltz* in you are adding a golden richness, a bubbling warmth, a loving tenderness, a promise of good things to come. Of course, some people will say that putting *schmaltz* in is "hamming it up." They should bite their tongues. Such people are bad actors. Better you should ignore them. I say you don't have to act like a frying pan to put some *schmaltz* in; you can act like people—good people; for the villains, no *schmaltz*.

If I tell you that *schmaltz* is rendered chicken fat, so don't be disappointed. You thought the way I'm talking it should be magic? A little magic it is. If it would be gold, it couldn't be so rich. If it would be perfume, it couldn't smell so good. When you put it in what's cooking, it not only has its own flavor but it brings out all the other flavors, too. Monosodium glutamate (such a word!) can be ashamed.

Now you are asking how to get *schmaltz*. If you'll continue reading, you'll see the recipe. The chicken fat you either get from the butcher or you cut it away from the chicken before you cook it and save up till you have from four–five chickens. If you don't want to go to the trouble (so why did you buy the book, it should cook for you yet?) you can buy from the kosher butcher ready–made *schmaltz*.

Whether you buy it or whether you make it, whether you are a musician, an actor, a cook, or just a plain person, my advice to you is ... put some *schmaltz* in.

SCHMALTZ AND GREBENES

chicken skin	**1 small onion, diced**
1 pound chicken fat	**1/4 cup water**

Cut chicken skin and fat into 1–inch squares. Place chicken fat, skin, onion, and water in a heavy saucepan over a very low flame. Simmer gently until all the fat has been rendered and the chicken skin is crisp and brown. Strain *schmaltz*. Drain *grebenes* (cracklings).

Note: Schmaltz is used for shortening and seasoning. *Grebenes* are used in chopped liver or *lokchen kugel* or eaten plain by *grebene* lovers.

♥ 7 ♥

So From Hunger
You Won't Starve

Mama used to say, "So long you got meat and potatoes, so from hunger you won't starve," and we didn't. Of course, sometimes you want a change and where will you find the time? You have to pick up from school the children. You have to take to dancing lesson, baseball, boy scout, girl scout. You're looking for a simple supper to make in a hurry. You think *milchiks* (dairy) is the answer? No. *Milchiks* when you are putting on the table looks simple. But it is not. It takes a lot of dairy dishes it should fill you up; but if you've got meat and potatoes, you've got already a whole meal. If you are lucky like me, you've got an electric stove so you put in the oven and forget till the bell rings to tell you dinner is ready. So when it is cooking you can go pick up from dancing and baseball.

If you are like I was, you worry that meat and potatoes will make you fat because they have calories. Don't worry. I'm not saying you will get thin, but fatter you won't get and it's all very scientific. This is how I learned.

I have a friend she's worried about her weight so she's making me go with her to lectures. So I go. While shall I wouldn't? I tell you it was worth the money. The professor is telling us about calories. Calories, he says, are measures of energy and if we are taking in more than we are putting out so we are gettting fat. He tells us something else. This I'm not sure I know how to explain. He calls it Specific Dynamic Action of Food and every food has it, except protein which has more of it. When you are eating pro-tein—which is meat—you are using up more energy di-gesting it than it is giving you ... 30 per cent more.

Now to me this is simple arithmetic. If I am going to a sale and I'm buying a $100 dress which it is reduced to $70, then I'm saving $30. If I'm saving $30, so I can afford to buy for $30 another dress which it was reduced from $50, or maybe I'm buying plain and simple a $30 dress, no reduc-tions because I can't afford to keep saving so much money on sales. Am I making myself clear?

So here are some recipes for meat. While you are saving 30 per cent calories on meat so you can afford to throw in a few potatoes. From where else will you get your energy? Science is a wonderful thing.

ESSIG FLAISH

3 to 4 pounds middle
　　cut of chuck
2 tablespoons *schmaltz*
4 onions, sliced
1 1/2 cups boiling water
1/2 teaspoon salt
1 bay leaf

3 peppercorns
dash of thyme
1/2 cup honey or 3/8
　　cup molasses
1 slice stale rye bread
juice of 2 lemons

Sear meat on all sides in hot fat in a Dutch oven or heavy skillet until evenly browned; pour off excess fat. Add onions, boiling water, salt, bay leaf, peppercorns, and thyme. Bring to a boil, then reduce heat. Cover and simmer until meat is almost tender (about 2 hours). Add honey or molasses, stirring it through the gravy. Soak rye bread in water. Mash it and add to gravy, mixing thoroughly. Add lemon juice. Cook uncovered 30 minutes, stirring occasionally. Serves 6 to 8.

GEDEMPTE FLAISH

2 onions, sliced	2 carrots, diced
2 cloves garlic, minced	1 1/2 teaspoons salt
3 tablespoons *schmaltz* or shortening	1 teaspoon paprika
	3 bay leaves
3 to 4 pounds middle cut of chuck	8 peppercorns
	1 cup tomato juice
1/2 green pepper, diced	2 tablespoons brown sugar
1 stalk celery, diced	

Einbren or thickening:
> 1 tablespoon flour
> 1 tablespoon *schmaltz* or shortening
> 1/2 cup meat stock

Brown onions and garlic in fat in a heavy skillet or Dutch oven. Remove the onions and brown the meat well on all sides. Return the onions to the skillet. Add the remaining ingredients. Bring to a boil, then reduce heat. Cover and simmer until the meat is tender (about 2 hours).

Heat a small skillet and place flour in it. Stir the flour constantly to prevent burning, until it is light brown—actually a sort of beige color. Remove from the flame. Stir 1 tablespoon fat into the flour until the mixture is smooth. Add meat stock, stirring until it forms a smooth paste. Stir thickening into the gravy and cook 15 minutes longer. Serves 6 to 8.

RUSSEL FLAISH

2 onions, sliced
1 clove garlic, minced
3 tablespoons *schmaltz*
　　or shortening
3 to 4 pounds beef
　　shoulder
1/4 cup water

2 tablespoons vinegar
1 tablespoon brown sugar
1/2 teaspoon salt
3 tablespoons catsup
2 bay leaves
1/2 cup seedless raisins
4 potatoes, quartered

Brown onions and garlic in fat in a heavy skillet or Dutch oven. Remove the onions. Brown the meat thoroughly on all sides, then return the onions to the skillet. Add all the remaining ingredients except the potatoes. Cover; reduce heat. Simmer for 1 hour. Add the potatoes. Simmer covered 1 1/2 hours longer. Serves 6 to 8.

SAUERBRATEN

4 pounds boneless chuck
1 1/2 cups red wine
2 cloves garlic, minced
1 tablespoon minced
　　onion
1/8 teaspoon thyme
1 tablespoon brown sugar

1 bay leaf
1 thin slice lemon
1/2 cup flour
1 teaspoon salt
schmaltz
1 cup boiling water

Place meat in a crock or deep bowl. Cover with a marinade made of wine, garlic, onion, thyme, sugar, bay leaf, and lemon. Cover and let stand in a cool place overnight. Remove meat from the marinade and wipe dry. Dredge on both sides with flour and salt. Dot the top with *schmaltz*. Place in an uncovered roasting pan in a 450–degree oven until the meat begins to brown (about 30 minutes). Add 1 cup of the marinade and 1 cup boiling water to the meat. Cover. Reduce heat to 350 degrees and cook until meat is tender (about 3 hours), basting occasionally. Serves 6 to 8.

SWEET AND SOUR MEAT BALLS

1 pound ground beef
1 onion, chopped
1 tablespoon bread
   crumbs
1 egg
1 teaspoon salt
pepper, to taste

1 tablespoons *schmaltz*
   or shortening
1 1/2 cups hot water
1 lemon, thinly sliced
1/4 cup sugar
1/4 cup seedless raisins

EINBREN OR THICKENING:
   1 tablespoon flour   **1/2 cup meat gravy**
   1 tablespoon *schmaltz*

Combine meat, onion, bread crumbs, egg, and seasonings. Form into small balls. Brown in *schmaltz* or shortening in a heavy skillet or Dutch oven. Add water, lemon, sugar, and raisins. Bring to a boil. Cover, reduce heat, and simmer about 45 minutes.

Heat a small skillet and place flour in it. Stir the flour constantly to prevent burning until it is a sort of beige color. Remove from heat. Stir 1 tablespoon fat into the flour until the mixture is smooth. Gradually stir in meat gravy to form a smooth paste. Add to meat and cook 5 minutes longer. Serves 4 to 6.

PIQUANT MEAT BALLS

2 pounds ground beef
1 egg
2 tablespoons bread
   crumbs
1 teaspoon salt

pepper, to taste
12 ounce bottle of chili
   sauce
6 ounces grape jelly
juice of 1 lemon

Combine meat, egg, bread crumbs, and seasonings. Shape into balls the size of a walnut. Heat chili sauce, jelly, and lemon juice in a heavy skillet or Dutch oven until blended Add the meat balls, cover, and simmer for 30 minutes. Uncover and cook 15 minutes longer, stirring frequently to prevent sticking. Serves 8 to 10.

HAMBURGERS DE LUXE

2 pounds ground beef
1 large onion, minced
1 egg
1/3 cup bread crumbs
1 teaspoon salt
pepper, to taste
2 tablespoons *schmaltz*
   or shortening

1 small can (8 ounce)
   tomato sauce
1 small can water
1/4 cup vinegar
1/4 cup brown sugar
10 whole cloves
1 bay leaf
10 gingersnaps, broken
   into bits

Combine meat, onion, egg, bread crumbs, salt, and pepper.
Form into thick patties. Fry in fat in a heavy skillet until
brown on one side. Turn. Add remaining ingredients and
bring to a boil. Reduce heat and let simmer until the sauce
thickens (about 45 minutes). Serves 8.

STUFFED VEAL BREAST

Have the butcher cut a pocket in a 5 pound veal breast. Rub
the meat and the cavity with garlic, and sprinkle salt and
pepper into the cavity. Fill evenly with stuffing, but do not
pack too tightly since the stuffing swells. Place meat on a
rack in an open roasting pan. Roast in a slow oven, 300
degrees, allowing 35 minutes per pound. Serves 8 to 10.

Bread Stuffing

Enough stale challah
   (Sabbath bread; see
   page 122) or white
   bread to make 3 cups
   when soaked and
   squeezed dry)
1 large onion, diced
1 green pepper, minced

1 carrot, shredded
3 tablespoons *schmaltz*
   or shortening
1/2 teaspoon salt
1/2 teaspoon garlic salt
dashes of ginger, paprika,
   and pepper
1 egg

Soak bread in water and squeeze dry. Saute onion, green
pepper, and carrot in fat. Combine all ingredients.

Apple Stuffing

1 large onion, diced	2 cups soft bread crumbs
3 tablespoons *schmaltz*	or bread that has
3 cups chopped apples	been soaked in water
1/2 teaspoon salt	and squeezed dry

Saute onions in *schmaltz* and combine with remaining ingredients.

BEEF TONGUE

3 to 4 pound beef tongue,	1 tablespoon vinegar
fresh or smoked*	6 whole cloves
boiling water	6 peppercorns

Place tongue in a deep kettle. Cover with boiling water. Add vinegar and seasonings. Bring to a rapid boil, then reduce heat and simmer until a fork will easily penetrate to the center of the tongue (3 to 4 hours). Let it stand in the water in which it has cooked until cool. Remove and peel off skin. Slice and reheat in sweet and sour sauce (see page 56). Serves 6.

Note: If smoked tongue is used, it should be soaked in cold water for several hours. Place in a kettle, cover with boiling water, and continue as directed above.

TONGUE WITH RAISIN SAUCE

3 to 4 pound beef tongue,	1 cup seedless raisins
smoked or pickled	1 cup prune juice

Cover tongue with water and boil until tender (3 to 4 hours). The tongue is tender when a fork will easily penetrate to the center. Change water several times during cooking if the tongue is salty. Remove skin. Place in a roasting pan. Add raisins, 1 cup water, and prune juice. Bake 1 hour at 350 degrees, basting frequently. Serves 6.

SWEET AND SOUR SAUCE

2 cups liquid in which
    tongue has cooked
1 large onion, diced
1 tablespoon *schmaltz* or
    shortening
1 tablespoons flour
1/2 teaspoon salt

1 stick cinnamon
4 whole cloves
1/4 cup chopped almonds
1/4 cup seedless raisins
1/4 cup brown sugar
1 tablespoon honey
juice of 1 lemon

Heat 2 cups of the liquid in which the tongue has cooked. Saute onion in hot *schmaltz* in a large, heavy skillet until golden. Sprinkle with flour. Slowly add hot tongue liquid, stirring constantly. Cook until smooth and slightly thickened. Add remaining ingredients. Simmer for 10 minutes, stirring constantly. Add sliced tongue and simmer until tongue is heated. Remove cinnamon before serving.

PRAAKES, HALISHKES, GALUPTZI, GEVIKELTE KRAUT, OR STUFFED CABBAGE

12 large cabbage leaves
boiling water
1 pound ground beef
1 small onion, grated
1/2 cup cooked rice
1/2 teaspoon salt
pepper, to taste

2 cups canned tomatoes
1/2 cup seedless raisins
1 onion, minced
2 tablespoons vinegar
2 tablespoons sugar
1/4 cup dark Karo syrup
gingersnaps

Soak cabbage leaves in boiling water while preparing the meat. Combine meat, onion, rice, salt, and pepper. Drain cabbage leaves. Place a portion of meat in each cabbage leaf; roll up and fasten with a toothpick. Place cabbage rolls in a large, deep kettle. Add all the remaining ingredients except the gingersnaps. If there is not enough liquid to cover rolls, add water just to cover. Bring to a boil and cook at a slow boil for 1 hour. Put a layer of gingersnaps over the tops of the cabbage rolls. Reduce heat and simmer 1 hour longer. Serves 6 to 8.

STUFFED CABBAGE WITH APRICOT PRESERVES

12 large cabbage leaves	1/2 teaspoon salt
boiling water	pepper, to taste
1 pound ground beef	1 28 ounce can tomatoes
2 tablespoons	juice of 2 lemons
uncooked rice	1/4 cup brown sugar
1 egg	1/2 cup apricot preserves
1 onion, minced	

Soak cabbage leaves in boiling water while preparing the meat. Combine meat, rice, egg, onion, and seasonings. Drain cabbage leaves. Place a portion of the meat mixture in the center of each cabbage leaf. Roll up and fasten with a toothpick. Place in a deep kettle. Cover with the remaining ingredients. It may be necessary to add more water just to cover. Bring to a boil, reduce heat, and simmer gently about 2 1/2 hours. Serves 6 to 8.

BRISKET AND BEANS

1 quart navy beans	2 teaspoons salt
2 pounds plate brisket	3/4 cup brown sugar
1 large onion, sliced	2 tablespoons molasses
2 teaspoons dry mustard	boiling water

Cover beans with cold water and soak overnight. Drain, cover with fresh water, and heat just to the boiling point. Drain beans. Place brisket, beans, and onion in a baked bean crock. Mix mustard, salt, sugar, and molasses with 1 cup boiling water. Pour over beans. Add boiling water to cover. Cover crock tightly. Bake covered at 250 degrees for 6 hours. Uncover and cook 1 hour longer. Serves 6 to 8.

KISHKE (STUFFED DERMA)

**9 feet of clean beef
    casings***
2 cups flour
1 cup matzo meal
1 1/2 teaspoons salt

1/4 teaspoon pepper
**1 cup melted *schmaltz*
    or chopped suet**
salt and pepper

Wash casings in cold water and cut into 12–inch lengths. Tie one end of each length tightly with white sewing thread. Turn casings inside out. Combine flour, matzo meal, seasonings, and *schmaltz* or suet. Fill each casing loosely with this stuffing and tie the remaining end. Drop into rapidly boiling water and boil 10 minutes. Drain.

When cool enough to handle, scrape fat off the casings with the dull edge of a knife. Drop into rapidly boiling water (about a gallon) to which has been added 1 tablespoon salt and at least 1 teaspoon pepper. Reduce heat and simmer uncovered for 3 hours. Remove from water. Brown for 1 hour around a roast or roasting poultry. Serves 9 or serves 8 with Papa getting an extra helping.

* Kosher butchers sell beef casings that have been well cleaned.

PUTCHA OR CHOLODYETZ

1 calf's foot
1 clove garlic
1 bay leaf
1 onion

**2 hard–boiled eggs,
    sliced**
lemon or parsley garnish

Have the butcher chop the calf's foot into quarters. Clean thoroughly. Soak in cold water for 1 hour. Drain. Place in a kettle, cover with water, and bring to a boil. Reduce heat and simmer for 2 hours. Add garlic, bay leaf, and onion. Simmer 1 hour longer. Remove calf's foot. Cut the meat from the bone into small bits. Arrange the meat bits and hard–boiled egg slices on a platter. Pour strained liquid over all. Chill until firm. Garnish with lemon slices and sprigs of parsley. Serve as an appetizer. Serves 6.

❤ 8 ❤

CHOLENT

I used to think cholent was cholent and there was only one, just like right is right and there are no two ways about it. I was wrong. There are as many cholents as there are cooks, so I have come to the conclusion that a cholent is any food that has the stamina to withstand 24 hours of cooking. The 24 hours of cooking is the common ingredient. This is necessary because no one wants to cook on the Sabbath, but everyone wants a hot meal. So cholents were invented they should stay in the oven from Friday afternoon until Saturday noon. This way everyone enjoyed and no one broke the Sabbath. This is like having your cake and eating it too.

CHOLENT

12 small potatoes
salt and pepper
flour
7 eggs

1 cup *schmaltz*
1 teaspoon sugar
4 pounds *brust*
 (boneless brisket)

Pare potatoes and roll in salt, pepper, and flour. Beat eggs with *schmaltz* and sugar. Add a pinch of salt and enough flour to make a very loose dough, just firm enough to handle. Place dough in a roaster. Put meat and potatoes around it. Cover with salted water; there should be 1 inch of water above the ingredients. Cover roaster and bake at 250 degrees for 24 hours. Serves 6 to 8.

LIMA BEAN CHOLENT

1 pound dried lima beans
3 pounds *brust*
 (boneless brisket)
salt, pepper, paprika,
 and ginger
3 onions, sliced
1 clove garlic, minced

1/4 cup *schmaltz* or
 shortening
6 potatoes or 1 cup
 uncooked barley
1 bay leaf
2 tablespoons flour
boiling water

Soak beans overnight. Drain. Rub meat with seasonings and brown it and the onions and garlic in fat. Place meat and onions in a baked–bean crock. Add beans, peeled whole potatoes or barley, and bay leaf. Sprinkle with flour. Add boiling water to cover. Cover the crock tightly and place in a 400–degree oven. After 30 minutes reduce heat to 250 degrees. Cook overnight. Serves 6 to 8.

❤ 9 ❤

TZIMMES AND A
GAHNTZE TZIMMES

*T*zimmes is a word impossible to translate. Ask anyone, "What is a *tzimmes*?" and you get the answer, "You don't know what a *tzimmes* is?" This is not very satisfactory, as you can see.

Now, I know very well what a *tzimmes* is, but do you think I was born yesterday? When you're looking for information so it pays to be ignorant. The people you are asking should feel you are even more ignorant than they are. This flatters them.

"If I knew, would I be asking?" I say. "So what is a *tzimmes*?"

"A *tzimmes* is ... why a *tzimmes* is a delicacy, a *maichel*. You could be even the President of the United States and you would enjoy a good *tzimmes*."

"Nu," I'm continuing, "so what is a *tzimmes*?"

The closest I have come to an answer is that a *tzimmes* is a mishmash. Now, a mishmash is a hodgepodge and a hodgepodge is ... not a *tzimmes*, believe me. A *tzimmes* is really more than a mishmash and better than a maichel. It's a big thing in anyone's life. A *gahntze tzimmes* is really something to boast about—a big production. For instance, from a good *tzimmes* a cook is entitled to make a *gahntze tzimmes*.

There is in the New York Public Library an expert on *tzimmeses*. He says a *tzimmes* is a dessert. Who am I to argue with an expert? However, in my opinion a *tzimmes* is a one-dish meal usually served as the fourth course in a six-course dinner.

A *tzimmes* can be made from almost any ingredient. From my wall–to–wall carpeting I could make a *tzimmes*, and from my new mink coat I am justified in making a *gahntze tzimmes*. In other words, from all these things I'm entitled a little bragging.

Of course, there are always some people who think not. You will find people who will begrudge you anything. They will say, "She got a mink coat so she's making from it a *gahntze tzimmes*. I knew her when she only had a Persian lamb."

From all these things you can make a *tzimmes*, but most *tzimmeses* are made from carrots.

CARROT TZIMMES

1 pound beef plate brisket	1/2 teaspoon salt
2 pounds carrots	3 tablespoons brown sugar

EINBREN OR THICKENING:
   2 tablespoons flour
   2 tablespoons *schmaltz* or shortening
   1 cup carrot stock

Simmer the brisket in water to cover until almost tender (about 1 1/2 hours). By this time the water will have boiled down to about half the original amount. Peel carrots and slice in 1/2–inch rounds. Add carrots, salt, and sugar to meat. Bring to a boil, reduce heat, and simmer until the carrots are very tender (about 45 minutes).

Brown flour in a very small skillet, stirring constantly to prevent burning. When flour is a very light brown, remove from flame. Add the *schmaltz* and stir until smooth. Gradually stir in the carrot stock to make a smooth paste. Add this paste to the carrots, stirring it in carefully. Continue to simmer until the stock has thickened (10 to 15 minutes). Serves 6 to 8.

TZIMMES WITH KNAIDEL OR HALKE

2 pounds *brust*
   (boneless brisket)
1 pound carrots
1 quart water
1 teaspoon salt

1 cup brown sugar
2 large sweet potatoes
3 large white potatoes
1/2 cup flour

Have the butcher cut the meat into 1 1/2–inch pieces. Peel carrots and slice in 1–inch rounds. Place meat and carrots in a deep kettle and add water, salt, and sugar. Bring to a boil, reduce heat, and simmer 1 hour. Skim. Place knaidel or halke (recipes follow) in the center of a Dutch oven or in a heavy iron kettle with a tight cover. Place the meat around the knaidel or halke. Drain the carrots and place them over the meat. Place sweet and white potatoes, peeled and cut in 1–inch rounds, over all. Make a thin paste by adding 1 cup water to 1/2 cup flour. Add 1 cup of meat–carrot stock and stir until smooth. Stir paste into remaining stock and pour over *tzimmes*. If necessary, add more boiling water to cover the tops of the potatoes. Cover. Bake at 325 degrees for 4 1/2 hours. Remove cover and cook 30 minutes longer. *Tzimmes*, a tossed salad, and dessert should make a hearty meal. Serves 4 heavy eaters or 6 light ones.

Note: This *tzimmes* looks so beautiful when done that it is a shame to remove it to a platter for serving. If you have an oversized party casserole, use it for baking and serving.

KNAIDEL

1/2 cup *schmaltz*
2 eggs, beaten
1 teaspoon salt

1 tablespoon sugar
1/4 cup warm water
3/4 cup matzo meal

Cream *schmaltz* and eggs. Stir in salt, sugar, and water. Add matzo meal and mix well. Refrigerate for about 30 minutes. The batter should be thick enough to form into one large ball. If necessary, add more matzo meal. Wet the hands when forming the batter into a ball.

HALKE

1 cup unsifted flour
1/2 teaspoon salt
1/2 teaspoon baking
   powder
2 teaspoons sugar

1/2 cup chopped beef
   suet
4 to 6 tablespoons cold
   water

Sift together dry ingredients. Stir in chopped suet. Add only enough water to hold the dough together. Shape into a large ball.

CARROT–SWEET POTATO TZIMMES

2 to 3 pounds top rib
   or boneless brisket
2 tablespoons *schmaltz*
boiling water
4 large sweet potatoes,
   diced

1 bunch carrots, sliced
   crosswise
1 teaspoon salt
dash of pepper
1/2 cup brown sugar

EINBREN OR THICKENING:
  2 tablespoons flour
  2 tablespoons *schmaltz*
  1 cup *tzimmes* stock

Sear meat on all sides in hot fat in a Dutch oven or heavy skillet until evenly browned; pour off excess fat. Add boiling water to cover. Cover skillet and simmer for 1 hour. Add carrots, salt, and pepper. Turn up flame and bring to a boil.

Cover, reduce heat, and simmer for 30 minutes. Add sweet potatoes and brown sugar. Cover and simmer for 1 hour.

Heat flour in a small skillet until pale brown, stirring constantly to prevent burning. Stir in *schmaltz*. Slowly add stock, stirring constantly. When smooth and thick, pour over *tzimmes*, shaking pot to distribute evenly.

Place in 350 degree oven until browned (about 1 hour). Serves 4 to 6.

PRUNE AND POTATO TZIMMES

1 pound uncooked
  prunes
2 pounds boneless
  brisket
1 onion, sliced
2 tablespoons *schmaltz*

4 large potatoes,
  quartered
1/2 teaspoon salt
1/2 teaspoon cinnamon
1/2 cup honey

EINBREN OR THICKENING:
  2 tablespoons flour
  2 tablespoons *schmaltz*
  1 cup *tzimmes* stock

Cover prunes with water and soak for several hours. Brown meat and onion in *schmaltz* in a Dutch oven or heavy skillet. Add potatoes, prunes, and the water in which the prunes have soaked. Cook uncovered over moderate heat for about an hour. Add salt, cinnamon, and honey. Cover partially so that some steam may escape. Simmer for about an hour. A little water may be added from time to time, but the gravy must be thick.

Heat flour in a small skillet until pale brown, stirring constantly to prevent burning. Stir in *schmaltz*. Slowly add *tzimmes* stock, stirring constantly.

When thickening is smooth, add to *tzimmes*, shaking the pot to distribute evenly. Simmer 10 minutes longer. Serves 4 to 6.

MEATLESS PRUNE AND POTATO TZIMMES

1/2 pound uncooked prunes
1 quart water
8 medium–sized whole potatoes, peeled
1/3 cup sugar
1 teaspoon salt

juice of 1/2 lemon
3 raw potatoes, grated but not drained
1/3 cup flour
2 tablespoons butter
1/2 teaspoon salt
dash of pepper

Cover prunes with water, bring to a boil, and remove from heat. Place 8 whole potatoes in a 3–quart greased casserole. Add prunes and the water in which they have cooked. Add sugar, salt, and lemon juice. Cover and bake at 350 degrees for 1 1/2 hours.

Mix together the grated potatoes, flour, fat, salt, and pepper, and spoon this mixture over the prunes and whole potatoes. Bake covered for 1 hour. Remove cover and continue baking until the top is reddish golden (30 minutes to 1 hour). Serves 8.

PRUNE AND RICE TZIMMES

1 cup uncooked prunes
1 quart water
1 cup rice or farfel
1/2 cup honey or
    brown sugar

juice and grated rind of
    1 lemon
1/2 cup butter
1/4 teaspoon of cinnamon
pinch of salt

Soak prunes for several hours in 1 quart water in the pot in which they are to cook. Add rice or farfel and bring to a boil. Reduce heat.

Add the remaining ingredients and simmer for 30 minutes. Brown under the broiler for a few minutes. Serves 6 to 8.

FRUIT TZIMMES

1 1/2 pounds mixed
    dried fruit (prunes,
    peaches, pears,
    apricots, raisins
1/2 cup brown rice

4 tablespoons honey
1/4 teaspoon cinnamon
1/2 teaspoon salt
2 cups boiling water

EINBREN OR THICKENING:
    2 tablespoons flour
    2 tablespoons butter or *schmaltz*
    1 cup water

Wash fruit in hot water; drain. Combine with rice, honey, seasonings, and water. Bring to the boiling point, then reduce heat and simmer slowly until the rice is tender (20 to 30 minutes). It may be necessary to add a little water.

Heat flour in a small skillet until light brown, stirring constantly to prevent burning. Stir in butter or *schmaltz*. Slowly add water, stirring constantly. When einbren is smooth and thick, add to fruit. Cook until the fruit liquid has thickened. Remove to a casserole and brown lightly under the broiler flame for a few minutes. Serve hot as a dessert. Serves 6 to 8.

A GAHNTZE TZIMMES

3 to 4 pounds *brust*
   (boneless brisket)
2 tablespoons *schmaltz*
3 large carrots
1/2 pound prunes
1/2 pound dried apricots
1 lemon, thinly sliced

3 large sweet potatoes
juice of 1 orange
5 cups boiling water
1 1/2 tablespoons
   brown sugar
2 tablespoons flour

Sear meat well in hot fat in a Dutch oven or heavy skillet on top of the stove. Transfer to a roasting pan. Peel carrots and cut in 1–inch round slices. Place them around meat. Add prunes, apricots, and lemon slices. Peel sweet potatoes and cut in 1–inch slices. Place over meat and fruit in the roaster.

Add orange juice to boiling water. Combine brown sugar and flour and add enough water to make a thin paste. Add this paste to the orange juice mixture. Pour over the *tzimmes*. If necessary, add more boiling water to bring liquid to the top of the *tzimmes*. Cover. Bake at 400 degrees for 1 hour. Reduce heat to 325 degrees and continue baking 4 1/2 hours. Uncover and bake 30 minutes longer. Serves 8 to 10.

How I Cook My Goose

Modesty is my greatest virtue. I never like to praise myself. "Let others praise me," I always say. This they are not always doing, but in one thing no one can deny my ability. That is why in this chapter I'm giving you my own private personal recipe how I cook my goose because I have yet to find anyone who can do it better. Now, I don't expect you just to take my word for it. Ask anyone who knows me—they'll tell you the same thing.

It happens quite often that I'm giving dinner parties, and my friends are enjoying. And let me tell you, what I overhear them saying does my heart good. It never happens after one of my parties that I shouldn't overhear my friends saying one to the other, "Did she cook her goose!" Such simple words of praise are what a good cook lives for.

So now I'm giving you directions how to cook your goose. Of course, to me it comes natural, but you can cook your goose good, too, if you try.

STEWED GOOSE

1 goose (about 8 pounds)
garlic
flour
salt and pepper

2 tablespoons *schmaltz*
   or shortening
2 cups boiling water
   or soup stock

Have butcher cut the goose into serving portions. Remove the skin and most of the fat. Rub pieces with garlic and dredge with flour seasoned with salt and pepper. Brown goose in hot fat in a Dutch oven or large skillet with a tight cover. Add boiling water or soup stock.

Cover and simmer gently 30 minutes per pound. Serve with sauce. Serves 8.

Sauce for the Goose (also for the Gander)

1 1/2 cups strained
   goose gravy
3 tablespoons sherry or
   Rhine wine
1 tablespoon cider
   vinegar

2 tablespoons flour
2 tablespoons melted
   schmaltz **or shortening**
4 tablespoons brown
   sugar
dash of nutmeg

Add wine and vinegar to goose gravy. Brown flour lightly in a small heavy skillet, stirring constantly to prevent burning. Stir in fat. Very gradually add 1/2 cup of the gravy, stirring until smooth.

Add this thickening to the remainder of the gravy. Add brown sugar and nutmeg. Simmer gently, stirring constantly until the sauce is smooth and slightly thickened.

ROAST GOOSE

1 goose (about 8 pounds)   **1/2 teaspoon ginger**
1 teaspoon salt   **flour**
1/2 teaspoon pepper

Stuff and truss goose. Prick the skin with a fork in several places. Sprinkle with salt, pepper, ginger, and flour. Place goose on a rack in an uncovered roasting pan. Roast at 325 degrees about 25 minutes per pound. Remove fat as it is rendered from the goose. Serves 8.

Apple Stuffing

5 tart apples   **1/2 teaspoon salt**
1 cup bread crumbs   **dash of pepper**
1/2 teaspoon poultry   **dash of nutmeg**
  seasoning

Peel, quarter, and core apples. Cook in a small amount of water until half done (10 minutes). Combine with remaining ingredients.

Potato Stuffing

2 cups mashed potatoes   **1 tablespoon melted**
4 tablespoons grated   ***schmaltz* or shortening**
  onion   **1 tablespoon minced**
1 egg, beaten   **parsley**
salt and pepper, to taste **1 teaspoon caraway seed**

Combine all ingredients. This amount of stuffing is for a 6–pound goose.

STEWED DUCKLING

duckling (about 4
　pounds), quartered
salt and pepper
2 tablespoons *schmaltz*
　or shortening
1 onion, sliced

1/2 cup boiling water
1/2 cup currant jelly
　or marmalade
1/2 cup sherry or Rhine
　wine
2 bay leaves

Sprinkle duckling with salt and pepper. Brown thoroughly in hot fat in a Dutch oven. Remove duckling to a platter. Brown onion in the same fat. Add jelly, wine, water, and bay leaves. Simmer gently until the jelly dissolves. Return duckling to the Dutch oven. Cover tightly and simmer gently until tender (about 2 hours), turning duckling occasionally. Remove duckling to a warm platter. Strain gravy and pour over duckling. Serves 4.

ROAST DUCK

Use a 5–pound duck. Sprinkle cavity with salt and pepper. Stuff and truss duck. Sprinkle with salt and pepper. Place on a rack in an uncovered roaster. Roast at 325 degrees about 25 minutes per pound, basting occasionally with the juice of 1 orange. Serves 4.

ROAST CHICKEN

Stuff and truss a young hen (about 5 pounds). Place in an open roaster in a 450–degree oven until browned (about 20 minutes). Add 1/2 cup boiling water; cover tightly. Reduce heat to 275 degrees and cook until tender (about 30 minutes per pound). Serves 6 to 8.

Bread Stuffing

4 cups stale bread, cubed
2 tablespoons *schmaltz*
　or shortening

1/8 teaspoon pepper
1/8 teaspoon ginger
1/4 teaspoon poultry

chicken heart and liver,
    boiled and chopped
1 teaspoon salt

seasoning
1 tablespoon minced
    parsley
1 egg, beaten

Soak bread in cold water and squeeze dry. Heat fat in a skillet. Add soaked bread and stir until all the fat is absorbed. Remove from flame. Add heart, liver, seasonings and parsley. Stir in beaten egg.

Note: To use as stuffing for duck, add 2 tablespoons orange juice and the grated rind of 1 orange.

CHICKEN POT ROAST

1 4–pound roasting hen
1/2 clove garlic
salt and pepper

2 cups hot water
1 onion, sliced
1 stalk celery, sliced

Rub chicken with garlic inside and outside. Sprinkle surface and cavity with salt and pepper. Place on a rack in a roasting pan. Roast in a 475–degree oven until browned (20 to 30 minutes). Add hot water, onion, and celery. Cover tightly and reduce heat to 350 degrees. When chicken is almost tender (about 1 hour), remove the cover and cook 30 minutes longer, basting occasionally. Serves 6.

STEWED CHICKEN

1 young stewing hen,
    4 to 5 pounds
1/4 cup *schmaltz* or
    shortening
3 sprigs parsley
3 celery tops

1 carrot, sliced
1 onion, sliced
2 teaspoons salt
1/8 teaspoon pepper
boiling water

Cut chicken into serving portions. Brown in fat in Dutch oven. Add remaining ingredients and boiling water to cover. Bring to a boil and boil for 5 minutes. Reduce heat and simmer until tender (about 2 1/2 hours). Serves 6 to 8.

CHICKEN GIBLETS WITH RICE

6 chicken giblets
  (gizzard, heart,
  and liver), diced
1 clove garlic, minced
2 tablespoons *schmaltz*
  or shortening

1/2 cup chopped nuts
1 1/2 cups uncooked rice
1 cup raisins
1 quart chicken stock
salt and pepper
1 tablespoon minced
  parsley

Saute giblets and garlic in hot fat in a Dutch oven. Add nuts, rice, and raisins. Cover with chicken stock and bring to a boil. Reduce heat; cover and simmer for 1 hour. Add salt and pepper to taste. Add parsley. Continue cooking until almost dry. Serves 6.

GEFILTE HELZEL

Remove skin in one piece from the neck of poultry. Stuff loosely with stuffing as for kishke (see page 58). Sew up both ends with white sewing thread. Bake with poultry until very brown.

❤ II ❤

GEHAKTE LEBER ORDINAIRE OR WITH SOCIAL STANDING

(TRANSLATION: CHOPPED LIVER, PLAIN OR FANCY)

I don't know when or where chopped liver originated, but I suspect it was first cooked up by Sam Levenson's mother when she asked the butcher to throw in a piece of liver for the dog.

Nowadays the price of calves liver alone should make *gehakte leber* a delicacy, but some people are ashamed of its lowly origin ... so go do them something. They won't stop eating it, but they must call it liver paté, liver paste (pheh!), or liver and egg salad. They've got to fancy it up so you shouldn't know what it really is. So you can call it what you want; you can make it look like pineapple; you can make it look like strawberries, red yet, but you can't fool me. I still say it's *gehakte leber*.

One cookbook calls it liver and egg salad and says you should mix in it French dressing in which *schmaltz* has been substituted for the olive oil. Pheh! Poison! For an orthodox chopped–liver lover like I am, this is desecration.

Now, my Mama believed in changing with the times. Other people know better, so do like other people. She came to America, so right away Mama adopted new customs— the Saturday–night bath, chicken every Sunday, and so on.

One morning just before the Passover seder, Mama said to me, "Make radish roses they should go around the *gehakte leber*." For so much progress I'm not. Would you put picture postcards around a Rembrandt? "Mama, for the *gehakte leber* I'm not making radish roses."

"Oi, such a stubborn child," said Mama. "Just like the Papa," and for three years she's not talking to me.

So this is the way I feel about *gehakte leber*. This is the way I grew up and this is the way I'll die. You can trim it, you can fancy it up, but I like *gehakte leber* it should look like and taste like *gehakte leber*. Go do me something.

Of course, there are all kinds of people in this world and who says that's bad? It just takes understanding. Everyone should know the way I feel about *gehakte leber*, and I should know how some people don't feel about it. So for those people who don't feel that way, I've got delicious recipes how to make *gehakte leber*, then how to change it it should look like liver paté or liver and egg salad or how to *qvetch* it out from an ice–cream dipper like in New York cafeterias or how to *patchke* it with the hands until it is shaped like a pineapple with sliced olives they should look like eyes and with on top pineapple leaves they should prick your hands when you are reaching for too much at a kockt'l party or like strawberries they should be rolled in paprika with a piece parsley on top.

MY MOTHER'S RECIPE FOR GEHAKTE LEBER

by Sam Levenson (By kind permission of the author)

My mother made *gehakte leber* mostly out of cuts even the cow never used: *milts* (spleen), *bock* (cheek), *harts* (heart), *loong* (lung). Add *a touch of liver* for flavor. Drench the entire mixture with warm chicken fat. Only one ingredient is essential—hungry children.

GEHAKTE LEBER

(Chopped liver)

1 pound liver (beef, calf, chicken, or goose)	**1 onion***
	salt and pepper, to taste
2 hard–boiled eggs	**2 tablespoons *schmaltz* (or more)⁺**

Place liver under broiler and broil until well done (about 10 minutes), turning once. Remove from broiler and cool. Remove skin and veins. Put liver, eggs, and onion through a food grinder, using the fine blade. Season with salt and pepper. Add *schmaltz*, working it through the liver with a fork. The liver should be moist enough to hold together; if necessary, add more *schmaltz*. Serves 8.

* *Note:* Some people prefer to sauté chopped onion in *schmaltz* before adding to liver.

⁺ I put in 2 spoons, however there are schmaltz lovers who put in more. If 2 spoons are good, what can it hurt to put in more?

GOOSE LIVER WITH GREBENES

1 pound goose livers	**1 cup *grebenes* (crack-**
salt and pepper, to taste	**lings; see page 48)**

Place liver under broiler and broil until well done (about 10 minutes), turning once. Remove. Cool. Put livers and *grebenes* through a food grinder, using the fine blade. Season to taste. Serves 8.

Note: It may be necessary to add a bit of *schmaltz* if there is not enough fat on the *grebenes* to moisten the liver.

LIVER AND EGG SALAD

**1/2 pound chicken
    livers, broiled
4 hard–boiled eggs
2 small onions**

**2 stalks celery, minced
salt and pepper, to taste
1 to 2 tablespoons
    schmaltz, melted**

Chop together livers, eggs, and onions in a wooden bowl. (They should not be as finely chopped as for *gehakte leber*.) Add celery. Season with salt, pepper, and melted *schmaltz*. Serve on a crisp lettuce leaf. Serves 4.

CHOPPED LIVER MOLD

Prepare as *gehakte leber* (see page 77), using twice the amounts listed. Press into a well–greased mold; chill. To unmold, dip the bottom of the mold in hot water for minute.

CHOPPED LIVER STRAWBERRIES

Prepare as *gehakte leber* (see page 77). Using about a tablespoon of chopped liver, mold into the shape of a strawberry. Roll in paprika and stick a bit of parsley in the top. Serve on a bed of watercress, or use as a garnish for other dishes. These strawberries are very pretty around a green jellied salad.

CHOPPED LIVER PINEAPPLE

Prepare as *gehakte leber* (see page 77), using twice the amounts listed. Shape the liver into the form of a pineapple and press slices of stuffed olives on the "pineapple" in regular rows. Place pineapple leaves on top.

❤ **12** ❤

FRIDAY IS FISH

Friday is fish, and fish is usually *gefilte*, especially on holidays. *Gefilte* means "filled" or "stuffed" and if you eat enough of it that is what you will be. Some people really love *gefilte* fish and others eat it only for the horseradish that goes on top.

Mama was always proud of her *gefilte* fish. She made it from yellow salmon and *buffle*. *Buffle*, I discovered many years later, is *buffalo*, at least that is what I thought until recently when I took a trip to New York. My friends when they heard I'm writing a Jewish cookbook asked me, "So how are you making your *gefilte* fish?" "Like Mama made," I answer them, "from yellow salmon and buffalo." "You mean from *buffle*?" they said.

Now, I thought I knew what is *buffle* but I don't want people should think because I'm writing a book I know everything, so I said, "What is *buffle*?" Would you believe it, they said that in New York, *buffle* is any kind of fish that is cheapest on the market. What the fishman doesn't want to throw away he calls *buffle* and sells greatly reduced. Another friend, also a New Yorker, takes exception. "This can't be so," says my friend, "because every summer my father used to go fishing and every summer he caught nothing but *buffle*."

"Your father," the others told her, "was such a sportsman that he didn't know one fish from another, so he called them all *buffle*."

From this you can draw your own conclusions, but I know that Mama made from buffalo and yellow salmon *gefilte* fish. The buffalo she used because it was a "fat" fish and the yellow salmon because it was "lean."

Now, you are going to tell me that your mama used two other kinds of fish. I won't say she was wrong. Everybody's mama makes from different fish and makes a little different way. This you will find not only with *gefilte* fish but with everything. I could make up from my head a recipe and if I looked long enough, I would find someone's mama who made it that way, but there is room in my book for only one *gefilte* fish, so I'll make it my way. If you want to make different you can, but remember that *for two pounds of fat fish you want one pound of lean fish*, and for every pound of fish you want one egg and one tablespoon matzo meal or cracker meal. So why do you waste your time reading ... so go already, make the fish for Friday.

GEFILTE FISH

2 pounds buffalo (see above)	3 tablespoons matzo meal, cracker crumbs, or cracker meal
1 pound whitefish or yellow salmon	fish heads, skin, and bones
2 medium–sized onions	

3 eggs, well beaten
2 teaspoons salt
1/4 teaspoon white
  pepper
1 teaspoon sugar

1 teaspoon salt
1/2 teaspoon pepper
pinch of sugar
1 carrot, peeled and
  sliced

Ask the fishman to fillet the fish for you, saving the heads, skin, and bones. Put fish and 1 onion through the food grinder, using the fine blade. The fish should be very finely ground. If necessary, put it through the grinder twice. Place fish in a wooden chopping bowl. Stir in eggs, 2 teaspoons salt, 1/4 teaspoon pepper, and 1 teaspoon sugar. Chop with a hand chopper while gradually adding water to make a soft mixture (about 1/3 cup). Stir in matzo meal or cracker crumbs. Mix thoroughly.

Place fish heads, skin, and bones in a large kettle. Add 2 quarts cold water, 1 teaspoon salt, 1/2 teaspoon pepper, and a pinch of sugar. Bring to a boil and boil for 30 minutes. While the fish heads are cooking, wet hands and form fish into balls the size of small apples. Take the kettle off the heat and remove the fish heads, skin, and bones from the water. Carefully place the fish balls in the same water. Add 1 whole onion and the sliced carrot.

There should be enough liquid to cover the fish; if necessary, add more water. Cover the kettle and bring to a rapid boil. Uncover and reduce heat. Simmer for about 2 1/2 hours until the stock has been reduced to less than half the original amount.

Carefully remove the fish to a serving platter. Strain the fish stock and pour as much of the strained stock over the fish as the platter will hold. Arrange carrots around the fish as a garnish. Cool and refrigerate until the stock jells.

Note: Gefilte fish is usually served with horseradish as a first course, before the chicken soup. This recipe should serve 8 people, but who can tell? Some people want to make a whole meal of it before they start on the soup and the chicken.

KENNEBEC SALMON

2 pounds Kennebec
　salmon
1 large onion, sliced
1 tablespoon vinegar
juice of 1 lemon

1 tablespoon sugar
　(about)
1/2 teaspoon salt
1 bay leaf
1/4 cup raisins
2 egg yolks, beaten

Place salmon and all other ingredients except egg yolks in a saucepan, cover with water, and cook until done (20 to 30 minutes).

Remove fish to a platter. Gradually pour hot fish stock into beaten egg yolks, stirring constantly. Pour sauce over the fish. Serve hot or cold. Serves 6.

SCHARFE FISH

3 pounds pike cut in
　2–inch slices
salt
1 quart water
2 tablespoons vinegar

1 teaspoon salt
1/4 teaspoon peppercorns
1 carrot, sliced
1 stalk celery, sliced
1/2 onion, minced

Sauce

1 tablespoon butter
1 tablespoon flour
1 cup fish liquid, strained

1 egg yolk beaten with
　2 teaspoons water

Salt fish well and refrigerate for several hours. Rinse in cold water. Boil together water, vinegar, salt, peppercorns, and vegetables for 10 minutes.

Add fish and bring to a boil again. Reduce heat and simmer until fish is done (about 20 minutes). Remove fish to a heated platter or keep in a warming oven while preparing the sauce.

Melt butter, add flour, and stir until smooth. Add strained fish liquid and cook until smooth (1 or 2 minutes), stirring constantly. Gradually add liquid to the beaten egg yolk, stirring constantly. Pour sauce over fish. Serve immediately or cool and refrigerate and serve cold. Serves 6 to 8.

SWEET AND SOUR FISH

2 to 3 pounds lake trout
salt
1 onion, diced
1 lemon, sliced
1 bay leaf
1/2 cup brown sugar

1/2 cup raisins
1/4 cup chopped almonds
8 gingersnaps, broken
into bits
1/2 cup vinegar

Cut fish in serving–size portions. Salt well and refrigerate for 1 hour. Rinse well in cold water. Add onion, lemon, bay leaf, brown sugar, raisins, and almonds to 3 cups water. Bring to a boil. Add fish and cook until fish is done (about 20 minutes).

Remove fish to a warm platter. Soak gingersnaps in vinegar, stir into fish stock, and cook until the sauce is smooth. Pour the sauce over the fish. Serves 6.

BAKED FISH STEAKS

2 pounds fish steaks
(halibut is best)
1/4 teaspoon celery salt
1/4 teaspoon pepper
1 onion, sliced

2 tablespoons flour
2 tablespoons butter
1 cup milk
1 teaspoon minced parsley

Season fish with celery salt and pepper. Arrange in a well–buttered baking dish. Cover with onion rings and sprinkle with flour. Melt butter in warm milk; do not boil. Pour over fish. Sprinkle with parsley.

Bake at 350 degrees until the milk is almost absorbed (about 30 minutes). Serves 4 to 6.

FISH MARINADE

3 pounds pike cut in
  2–inch slices
head of pike
3 large onions, sliced
1 cup white wine
1/2 cup white vinegar

1/2 cup lemon juice
3 bay leaves
1 teaspoon whole mixed
  spices
1 teaspoon peppercorns

Salt fish well, refrigerate for several hours, and rinse lightly in cold water. Cover fish and fish head with water and cook until done (about 20 minutes). Remove fish head. Place fish in a crock with alternate layers of sliced raw onions. Boil 2 cups fish stock with wine, vinegar, lemon juice, bay leaves, spices, and peppercorns for 5 minutes. Strain hot liquid over the fish and onions. Cover the crock tightly and store in the refrigerator for at least 24 hours. The liquid will jell. This may be kept in the refrigerator for several weeks. Serves 8.

SALMON MARINADE

2 pounds salmon steaks
1 teaspoon salt
1 cup white wine
1/2 cup white vinegar

1/2 cup lemon juice
1 teaspoon whole mixed
  spices
5 peppercorns

Cover salmon steaks with salted water and boil until done (about 20 minutes). Remove fish to a platter. Cool. Boil 2 cups fish stock with wine, vinegar, lemon juice, spices, and peppercorns for 5 minutes. Strain, pour over cooled fish, and chill. Serves 4 to 6.

SCHMALTZ HERRING

Wash herring thoroughly under cold running water. Remove head, fins, and tail. Split down the belly and remove the entrails; rinse the inside thoroughly. Soak for several hours in cold water to cover. Slice and serve with hot potatoes boiled in their jackets, or season with white vinegar diluted with a little water.

Note: Herring odor can be removed from the hands by rubbing with a little cooking oil. Now all you need to know is how to remove the oil.

PICKLED HERRING

3 miltz herrings	10 peppercorns
2 onions, sliced	1 lemon, sliced
3 bay leaves	1 cup white vinegar
1 teaspoon whole	1/4 cup water
mixed spices	1 tablespoon brown sugar

Wash herrings carefully under cold running water. Remove heads, fins, and tails. Split down the bellies and remove the entrails; rinse the insides well. Soak for several hours in cold water to cover. Slice herrings in 1–inch slices and place in a 1–quart jar. Add onions, bay leaves, spices, peppercorns, and lemon slices. Bring vinegar, water, and sugar to a quick boil. Remove from heat and let stand until lukewarm. Add to the herring jar. Cover the jar and shake well to distribute the spices evenly. Let stand in the refrigerator at least 24 hours. Serve as an appetizer.*

*Note: As an appetizer, this should serve 6. But of course there are always people who want to make a meal of it, with hot boiled potatoes and cucumbers with sour cream and pumpernickel bread and butter.

HERRING AND POTATOES

3 miltz herrings	bread crumbs
5 potatoes	butter
2 onions, sliced	

Wash, clean, and soak herrings according to directions for *Schmaltz* Herring (page 84). Skin herrings and remove the backbones. Boil potatoes in their jackets until done. Peel and slice in 1–inch slices. Place a layer of sliced potatoes in a well–buttered casserole or baking dish. Alternate with layers of herring and onion slices, ending with a layer of potatoes. Sprinkle with bread crumbs and dot with butter. Bake at 425 degrees for 30 minutes. Serves 6.

BAKED HERRING

2 miltz herrings	1/4 cup brown sugar
1 onion, thinly sliced	1 bay leaf
3/4 cup white vinegar	8 peppercorns
1/4 cup water	flour

Wash, clean, and soak herrings according to directions for *Schmaltz* Herring (page 84). Place herrings in a glass baking dish and cover with slices of onion. Combine vinegar, water, and sugar; stir until the sugar dissolves. Pour over herrings. Add bay leaf and peppercorns and sprinkle with flour. Bake at 375 degrees for 20 to 30 minutes or until the onion is tender. Serves 4.

BAKED HERRING WITH CREAM

2 large miltz herrings	butter
4 onions, sliced	1/4 cup cream

Wash, clean, and soak herrings according to directions for *Schmaltz* Herring (page 84). Skin herrings; split them down the belly and remove entrails and backbones. Place herring fillets in a well–buttered glass baking dish. Boil onions for 5 minutes, drain, and place over the herrings. Dot with butter. Bake at 375 degrees until the onions are light brown (about 15 minutes). Add cream and bake 10 minutes longer. Serves 4.

CHOPPED HERRING

1 *schmaltz* herring	2 slices of challah
1 miltz herring	(Sabbath bread; see
2 small onions	page 122) or other
2 hard–boiled eggs	white bread
1 tart apple, pared and	pepper, to taste
cored	1 tablespoon mayonnaise
vinegar	(or less)

Clean, wash, and soak herrings according to directions for *Schmaltz* Herring (page 84). Skin. It is not necessary to bone the fish. Put herrings, onions, hard–boiled eggs, and apple through the food grinder, using the fine blade. Soak bread in vinegar and squeeze dry. Add to herrings, mixing thoroughly. Add pepper and mayonnaise. Serve as an appetizer on a crisp lettuce leaf or as a canapé on rounds of toasted rye bread. Serves 4.

❤ 13 ❤

EDUCATION IS A WONDERFUL THING

Education is a wonderful thing and I'm the first one to say it! But sometimes it gets a little confusing. Just when you learn something, education continues on and you have to learn something else which is maybe contradicting the first thing you learned.

Was a time when meat and potatoes was enough. Who wouldn't be glad for meat and potatoes? You gave the baby a good hard bagel to teethe on, and when the teeth came in, so it was meat and potatoes with every now and then a little bite herring, a piece kosher salami, it should develop a taste for the good things. So what? Just when you teach the baby it should sit at the table and eat real food like a human being, comes along baby food in jars. It looks like if food has a taste, so it's no good for babies. Till you bring up a boy he should know what good food is, so he is already married and his wife can't cook anyway, so better he shouldn't know what good food is in the first place than you should ruin a happy marriage.

The time mothers are learning that they have to feed the baby from jars, so they are learning also about vitamins. Now when the father is coming home he's not asking, "How much did baby eat today?" he's asking, "How many vitamins did baby get?" And it is not enough the baby should get his vitamins from cod-liver oil which it smells up the baby and the house and puts spots on your dress if it spills which you can't take it out. So where do you get vitamins? ... from vegetables. Potatoes is a vegetable, no? No. Potatoes is starch, so that's not counting.

And it is not enough just vegetables. According to the doctors and the professors, you have to have green vegetables and yellow vegetables, leafy vegetables and bulky vegetables, so when you are putting a dinner on the table it is not just something to eat. It's a regular moving picture ... in Technicolor.

This isn't all. Just when you think you know all about vitamins and how to feed the children they should get fat and healthy, along come psychologists and say "No." Education is always one step ahead. Psychologists say now that you can give a child vitamins with green vegetables and yellow ones, red ones even, and he'll stay thin. So what makes him fat? It's love.

One day I'm coming home late and I'm saying, "Children, Mama was late at a bridge game which she made a grand slam and she didn't have time to cook dinner. Come, I'll give you all a kiss." It didn't work. I had to quick make salami and eggs and open up a can peas.

If you are old-fashioned and you think love is not enough, so keep reading and I've got for you recipes how to cook vegetables. If you don't have time to cook a green vegetable and a yellow one, a thin one and a bulky one, so don't worry. Your child will do all right on *Love and Knishes.*

SAVORY BEETS

1 tablespoon butter	1/4 teaspoon salt
1 tablespoon flour	1 teaspoon ground ginger
1/2 cup beet liquid	1/8 teaspoon dry mustard
1 tablespoon vinegar	2 cups canned beets,
2 tablespoons brown sugar	shredded

Melt butter in a large saucepan. Add flour, stirring until smooth. Gradually add beet liquid, stirring constantly to keep smooth. Add remaining ingredients.

Cook until the sauce thickens slightly (5 to 10 minutes). Serves 4 to 6.

SWEET AND SOUR GREEN BEANS

1 pound green beans	1 heaping tablespoon *schmaltz*
1/2 teaspoon salt	
pepper, to taste	2 heaping tablespoons brown sugar
1 bay leaf	
1 heaping teaspoon whole cloves	2 tablespoons vinegar

Wash green beans and cut in desired lengths. Cover with water and bring to a boil. Add salt, pepper, bay leaf, and cloves. Reduce heat and cook at a slow boil until almost tender (about 20 minutes). Add *schmaltz*, brown sugar, and vinegar. Continue cooking until beans are tender (about 10 minutes). Serves 6.

SÜSSE FASOLYES (SWEET LIMAS)

1 1/2 cups dried lima beans	1 teaspoon salt
	1/2 cup honey

Cover beans with cold water and soak overnight. Drain, cover with cold water, and add salt. Bring to a boil in a covered saucepan. Reduce heat and simmer for 1 hour. Add honey. Cook uncovered until beans are tender and golden brown (about 1 hour). Serves 6 to 8.

BAKED LIMAS

2 cups dried lima beans	2 tablespoons *schmaltz*
1 1/2 quarts water	or butter
1 teaspoon salt	1/2 cup tomato catsup
pinch of sugar	

Bring limas to a boil in water. Add salt and sugar. Reduce heat and cook slowly until lima beans are very tender (about 1 1/2 hours). Drain beans. Place in a 2-quart greased casserole. Stir in *schmaltz* or butter and catsup. Bake at 350 degrees until limas are delicately browned and crusty on top (about 1 hour). Serves 6 to 8.

SWEET AND SOUR RED CABBAGE

1 medium-sized red cabbage, shredded	2 tablespoons sugar
1 tart apple, pared and sliced thin	1/2 teaspoon ground allspice
2 cups boiling water	1 teaspoon salt
	5 tablespoons vinegar

EINBREN OR THICKENING:
   1 tablespoon melted *schmaltz* or butter
   1 tablespoon flour
   1/2 cup cabbage liquid

Cook all ingredients together except thickening for 15 minutes. Make a paste by adding melted *schmaltz* or butter to flour. Stir until smooth. Slowly add hot cabbage liquid, stirring until smooth. Add the sauce to the cabbage and cook 10 minutes longer. Serves 6 to 8.

SWEET AND SOUR RED CABBAGE WITH GRAPE JUICE

1 small onion, chopped	2 tablespoons vinegar
1 tablespoon *schmaltz* or butter	2 tablespoons brown sugar
1 cup grape juice	4 cups shredded red cabbage
1 teaspoon salt	

Saute onion in *schmaltz* or butter until light brown. Add remaining ingredients. Simmer for about 30 minutes or until tender. Serves 8.

CHATZILIM* (EGGPLANT AUBERGINE)

1 eggplant large enough to make about 1 cup of pulp	salt and pepper, to taste
	1/2 onion, finely chopped
juice of 1/2 lemon	2 tablespoons mayonnaise or olive oil

Place eggplant above an open flame and let it actually burn on all sides until soft. Cool and peel. Mash pulp with a fork until it is like a paste. Add onion, salt, pepper, and lemon juice.

Stir in mayonnaise or olive oil or 1 tablespoon of each. Mix well. Serve on a lettuce leaf as an appetizer. Garnish with slices of tomato and cucumber. Serves 6 to 8.

* Recipe from the Embassy of Israel.

KASHA

1 1/2 cups medium-sized buckwheat groats
2 eggs
3 cups boiling water

1 teaspoon salt
1 onion, diced
4 tablespoons *schmaltz* or butter

Place groats in a shallow baking tin or lightly greased pie pan. Stir in eggs (do not beat) until all the grains are coated. Bake in a 350 degree oven, leaving the oven door open slightly.

Bake until all the grains are dry (about 20 to 25 minutes). Shake pan and stir groats about every 5 minutes to keep them from sticking. Transfer groats to a large saucepan. Add boiling water and salt.

Cover and cook over a moderate flame for 10 to 15 minutes. It may be necessary to add a little more water. When done, groats are tender, doubled in bulk, and all the cooking water is absorbed.

Saute onion in hot *schmaltz* or butter until brown. Add onion and fat to the groats. Serves 6.

Note: Kasha is a delicious accompaniment to roast chicken or pot roast; season with onions and chicken gravy or pot-roast gravy. Omit onion and fat if serving in chicken soup or as a cereal.

FALAFEL* (CHICK PEAS)

1 pound dried chick peas
3 slices white bread
2 canned hot cherry peppers
2 or 3 sprigs parsley

3 eggs, beaten
garlic powder, salt, and pepper, to taste
peanut oil for frying

Soak peas for 12 hours in cold water. Remove skins and grind peas with bread, peppers, and parsley. Add eggs and seasonings. Let stand 1 hour.

Make into balls about the size of a silver dollar (1 1/2 to 2 inches), round but flat enough to fry. Fry in deep oil (a sweet type such as peanut oil, not olive oil). Serve hot with sauce. Serves 6.

*Recipe from the Embassy of Israel.

Falafel Sauce

1 can (8 ounces) tomato sauce	**salt, to taste**
1 hot pepper, ground	**parsley garnish**

Mix ingredients and bring to a boil.

FISH POTATOES

potatoes	**1 teaspoon or more fresh**
fish stock	**ground black pepper**

Pare and quarter potatoes. Cook until done (about 20 minutes) in fish stock to which the pepper has been added. Serve hot, as a vegetable with a fish dinner.

POTATOES AND ONIONS

12 small new potatoes, peeled	**1 small onion, minced**
	1/8 pound butter

Boil potatoes in salted water until done (about 20 minutes). Place butter and minced onion in a serving bowl.

Add potatoes. As the butter melts, turn the potatoes so they become coated with the butter and onions. Serves 4 to 6.

Note: New potatoes are also good served with butter and 1/2 cup sour cream (omit onion).

POTATOES WITH CARAWAY SEEDS

12 small new potatoes	salt, to taste
3 tablespoons *schmaltz* or butter	1 teaspoon caraway seed

Boil potatoes in their jackets until done (about 20 minutes). Peel while still hot. Melt fat in a skillet. Add potatoes and brown well on all sides. Sprinkle with salt and caraway seed. Serves 4 to 6.

POTATO LATKES (PANCAKES)

2 cups grated raw potatoes (measure after draining)	1 rounded or heaping tablespoon flour or matzo meal
2 eggs, beaten	pinch of baking powder
1 teaspoon salt	1 small onion, grated (optional)

Combine all ingredients. Mix well. Drop pancake mixture by the tablespoonful onto a hot skillet generously greased with butter or shortening. (If you like thin, crisp pancakes, flatten with the back of a spoon.)

Fry on both sides until brown. Serve piping hot with sour cream, or with apple sauce as an accompaniment to a pot roast.

Note: This recipe should serve 4 to 6 people, but when some people see potato latkes they act like they haven't eaten for a week. They will want to make from latkes alone a meal. When you have people who enjoy so much, so you won't mind grating potatoes all day long.

POTATO LATKES WITH GREBENES

6 medium-sized potatoes
2 eggs, beaten
1/2 cup finely chopped
  grebenes **(see page 48)**
1/2 cup matzo meal
1 teaspoon salt
shortening for deep-frying

Peel, grate, and drain potatoes. Add eggs, grebenes, matzo meal, and salt. Mix well. Drop batter by the tablespoonful into hot shortening deep enough to cover the pancakes. Brown on both sides over moderate heat. Serves 4 to 6.

PAPRIKA SAUERKRAUT

2 large onions, diced
1 tablespoon *schmaltz*
  or shortening
1 tablespoon flour
1 28 ounce can sauerkraut
1 10-1/2 ounce can con-
  densed tomato soup
2 teaspoons paprika
2 tablespoons sugar
2 cups water

Brown onions in *schmaltz* or shortening. Sprinkle with flour and stir until well blended and smooth. Combine with remaining ingredients and simmer slowly for about 1 hour. Serves 4.

SWEET AND SAUERKRAUT

1 pound plate brisket
1 pound bulk sauerkraut
1 28 ounce can tomatoes
3 tablespoons brown
  sugar (or more)

Cover meat with water and cook uncovered in a large saucepan for 1 hour. Skim. Add sauerkraut, tomatoes, and sugar. Simmer uncovered for 2 hours. Serve with roast chicken or duck. Serves 6.

KISHUIM* (SQUASH)

1 onion, minced
1/8 pound butter
4 yellow squash (such
    as crook neck),
    peeled and cut in
    2-inch slices

5 tablespoons uncooked
    Minute Rice (optional)
    1/2 teaspoon salt
1 tomato, sliced
dash of pepper
1 teaspoon lemon juice

Saute onion in butter until golden. Add tomato, squash, and Minute Rice. Cover and cook over low flame until squash is soft (about 20 minutes). Season with salt, pepper and lemon juice. Serves 4 to 6.

*Recipe from the Embassy of Israel.

❤ 14 ❤

PAPA CALLED IT GRASS

If you think in this chapter I'm going to give you a lot of recipes how to make salads, so you couldn't be more wrong. In my home, we didn't know from salads except potato salad. Someone taught Mama how to make potato salad, so every Sunday every summer we had potato salad it should go with the fried chicken in a basket to "the park." Every Sunday we carried the basket to the streetcar. I don't know why. It was big enough to carry us.

In the basket besides the silver and dishes (who had paper plates?) was enough food to feed an army so that just in case anyone should be too lazy or too stingy to bring a big basket Mama could say, "So take from me. You welcome to it."

All day we would stay at the park. Where else can you have such a good time all day and it shouldn't cost any money? At night was even a free picture show—open air, not drive–in. After the picture show we would take the last car home. Everyone took the last car. Everyone was tired and wanted to get home. The motorman wanted to get home, too. He would clang the bell and send the car racing forward, up and down, and from side to side all at one time. The car was so packed with people and baskets that we didn't have room to shake around in. Once we had room. That was when the streetcar, the swings, the teeter–totters, the chicken, and the potato salad was for me too much.

I started to tell you about salads. I remember the first time we had in the house lettuce. Papa called it grass and he said in Yiddish, "This is strictly for the cows."

In our home, we didn't know from vitamins. Oranges we got once a year, on Passover, and we shouldn't eat too much the expensive oranges, we should save for company, so if I wanted an orange I had to visit where I would be company. Nowadays, if a child doesn't have its orange juice every day, the mother thinks, God forbid, it will get scurvy right away and she's calling up the doctor.

Like I was saying, we didn't know from vitamins just like we didn't know from allergies. Allergies ... a new word. Nowadays, as soon as an infant learns to talk, it knows already from allergies. So now instead of saying, "I hate spinach," they tell you, "So sorry, but I'm allergic to it."

I can imagine what Mama would have said about allergies: "Crazy! From eating you get sick? From not eating you get sick—you get consumption of the lungs, you get abnemia of the blood."

When it came to food, Mama had a saying: "A healthy person you give, a sick person you offer." But salads she didn't give and didn't offer. So if you want recipes how to make salads, buy yourself a good American cookbook and enjoy. But my feeling is: vitamins, shmitamins, as long as you're healthy.

CUCUMBER SALAD

2 large cucumbers
1 large onion
1/2 cup vinegar

1/2 cup water
1 teaspoon salt
2 tablespoons sugar

Pare and slice cucumbers thinly. Slice onion into thin rings. Place in a bowl with the cucumbers. Bring remaining ingredients to a boil. Pour over cucumbers and onions. Refrigerate until ready to serve. Serves 4 to 6.

FARMER'S CHOP SUEY*

2 cucumbers, thinly sliced
1 bunch radishes, sliced
1 bunch scallions, sliced

salt and pepper, to taste
1 pound cottage cheese
1 pint sour cream

Combine all vegetables in a bowl. Season to taste. Add cottage cheese. Top with sour cream. Serves 4 to 6.

* Where this name came from, I don't know. I was eating this salad long before I saw it listed this way on restaurant menus. Farmer's Chop Suey served with pumpernickel bread and butter could make a complete summer lunch.

EGG SALAD

6 hard–boiled eggs
1 small onion, diced

salt and pepper, to taste
schmaltz

Chop eggs. Add diced onion. Season to taste. Using a fork, work in just enough *schmaltz* to moisten. Serves 4.

❤ 15 ❤

AND IT CAME TO PASSOVER

Whand you are writing a cookbook, so you are hearing all the time remarks, "This is not like Mama made it." If you're not hearing it so much for plain everyday cooking, you are hearing when it comes Passover because maybe people are forgetting Mama's everyday cooking, but her Passover cooking they are not forgetting.

Passover is the holiday which it is supposed to commemorate the freeing of the Hebrews from slavery in Egypt, but the way it is observed you would think it celebrates the birth of the *knaidel* or matzo ball. To those people who say, "My Mama made it different," what can you answer? To these people I can only tell the story of some young friends of mine.

Newlyweds they were. Just married. You think this is the story about how the bride couldn't cook? So you're wrong. She was a good cook. Even her husband said, "Honey, you're a wonderful cook." This is good, no? But like most husbands, he didn't know how to leave well enough alone, so he adds, "But if you could only make *knaidlech* like Mama used to make."

Nu, she was a young bride; she wanted to please her husband, so she said, "Honey, if you want *knaidlech* like your Mama used to make, I'll learn to make them." You think this was easy? No. She went to all her friends and asked how to make *knaidlech*.

"You don't know how to make *knaidlech*?" they said. "It's very easy. You put in egg, you put in *schmaltz*, you put in matzo meal, and you got *knaidlech*."

"How much do you put in?" she wanted to know, and the answer she always got was, "You put in how much you want. You want a lot, you put in a lot. You don't want so much, you don't put in so much." From this she is not learning how to make *knaidlech*.

One day a friend says to her, "You'll never learn this way. You have to watch someone make them. Come to my home. I'll show you." So she went to her friend's home and watched her put in egg and *schmaltz* and throw in a handful of matzo meal. The *knaidlech* were cooked. They were delicious. She ran home right away to make *knaidlech*. You think she made them right? No. For five days she tried and failed. Finally it comes to her why her *knaidlech* are failures—her hand is not the same size as her friend's. So she runs right away to her friend with a measuring cup and says, "Throw in a handful matzo meal."

This time her *knaidlech* are perfect ... light as a feather. She could hardly wait until her husband came home to eat.

She served the knaidlech. She watched while he took the first bite. She watched him take the second bite.

"Well?" she asked.

"Well what?" he answered.

"The *knaidlech*," she said, "how are the *knaidlech*?"

"Oh, the *knaidlech*," he answered. "They're all right."

"All right?" she said. "What do you mean, 'all right'?"

"What do you mean what did I mean all right? I mean all right."

"Are they like your mama used to make?"

"Honey," he said, "they're all right, but don't get mad, they're not like Mama used to make."

Angry she was, but do you think she gave up? No. She says to him, "Darling, I love you and if you want *knaidlech*, *I'll give you knaidlech!*" And she did ... every day for six months.

One day she was making the *knaidlech* a misfortune happened—the bottom fell out of the matzo–meal box. All the matzo meal fell into the *knaidlech*. Well, I don't have to tell you, this made the *knaidlech* hard like rocks and heavy like lead, but my friend was already not so newlywed so she said to herself, "He'll eat these *knaidlech*."

Her husband took one bite of the *knaidlech* and said, "AH HAH! This is *mechiah*." For those who don't know I'll explain that a *mechiah* is a feeling something like the feeling you get when you take off a girdle that you've been wearing all day.

"This is a *mechiah*," said the husband. "Now *this* is the way Mama used to make them."

So if you'll read this chapter you'll find recipes how to make *knaidlech* or matzo balls, but I don't know if it's like your mama made.

MATZO BALLS
THE WAY I MAKE THEM

You want to know how I make matzo balls? I'll tell you. I put in *schmaltz*, I put in egg, and I put in matzo meal. How much? For every 2 tablespoons *schmaltz* (it shouldn't be melted) I drop in an egg, 1/2 teaspoon salt, a dash nutmeg, 1 tablespoon minced parsley, and I cream it together it should be smooth. Then I put in matzo meal until it gets thick but not dry—this is from 1/4 to 1/2 cup. Then I put in the refrigerator for 1 hour. Who has time to separate eggs and make such a tzimmes out of it? That is for cooks who cook from a book. Of course, if you have to cook from a book, it should be from my book. This makes 8. Serve two matzo balls per person. Matzo balls are usually served in clear chicken soup, but they can also be eaten as an accompaniment to a roast or poultry.

MATZO BALLS

6 eggs, separated   **1 cup matzo meal**
1 teaspoon salt   **2 tablespoons melted**
1/8 teaspoon pepper   ***schmaltz***

Beat egg whites until stiff. Beat egg yolks until light. Add salt, pepper, and melted *schmaltz* to beaten yolks; fold into egg whites. Fold in matzo meal one spoonful at a time. Refrigerate for at least 1 hour. Wet the hands and form batter into balls the size of a walnut. Drop into rapidly boiling soup or water. Reduce heat and cook slowly, covered, for about 30 minutes. Serves 12.

INSTANT MATZO BALLS

3 eggs, separated   **1/2 teaspoon pepper**
3/4 cup matzo meal   **1 1/2 tablespoons melted**
1 teaspoon salt   ***schmaltz***

Beat egg whites until stiff. Beat egg yolks until light yellow. Fold beaten yolks into whites. Fold in matzo meal, salt, and pepper. Stir in melted *schmaltz* and let stand 5 minutes. Drop from a tablespoon into rapidly boiling soup or water. Cook for 15 minutes. Remove one ball and test to see if it is cooked thoroughly. If not, continue to cook 5 minutes longer. Serves 8.

MARROW MATZO BALLS

2 heaping tablespoons marrow	2 heaping teaspoons minced parsley
1 egg	1/8 teaspoon ginger or nutmeg
1 heaping tablespoon minced onion	1/2 teaspoon salt
1 tablespoon *schmaltz*	1/4 to 1/2 cup matzo meal

Buy a large marrow bone from the butcher and scoop out the marrow with a knife. Drop marrow into a small bowl filled with ice water. Gently press marrow with the fingers until all the blood is out and the marrow is white. (This is a lot of trouble, but the result justifies it.) Place marrow in a small mixing bowl and cream it until it is about the consistency of mayonnaise. Add egg and continue creaming.

Saute onion in *schmaltz* until golden. Add parsley; sauté 1 minute longer. Add onion, parsley,*schmaltz*, and seasonings to the marrow mixture. Slowly add matzo meal until the mixture is thick but not dry. Try to use as little matzo meal as possible.

Refrigerate for 1 hour. Wet the hands and roll the batter into tiny balls the size of marbles. (They will triple in size when cooked.) Drop into simmering chicken soup and simmer for about 15 minutes. This makes about 24 balls, or enough for 6 people (four to each serving). Of course, everyone will ask for more, but don't give. They should have room for the rest of the dinner.

MATZO BALLS WITHOUT SCHMALTZ

3 eggs, separated   **1/2 teaspoon salt**
3/4 cup matzo meal

Beat egg whites until stiff. Beat egg yolks until light yellow and fold yolks into the whites. Fold in matzo meal. Refrigerate for at least 1 hour. Wet the hands and form mixture into balls the size of a walnut.

Drop into rapidly boiling water and cook about 20 minutes. Test one to see if it is cooked thoroughly; if not, continue cooking 5 minutes longer. Serves 8.

Note: Since no *schmaltz* is used, these can be served with dairy dishes or as a cereal in hot milk with a little butter.

CHAROSIS

2 tart apples   **1 teaspoon honey**
1/4 cup nuts (preferably   **1 tablespoon Passover**
**   walnuts)**   **wine**
1/4 teaspoon cinnamon

Pare and core apples. Chop apples and nuts together finely. Add cinnamon, honey, and wine. Serves 10 to 12. (This makes about 2 cups; serve 1 teaspoon to 1 tablespoon per person, on matzos.)

* Note: Charosis is served at the Passover seder as a symbol of the mortar and bricks that the Hebrews were forced to make for the pyramids and cities of Egypt.

FRIED MATZOS

6 matzos   **1/2 teaspoon salt**
4 eggs   **butter**
1/2 cup water

Break matzos into quarters and soak in cold water until softened. Gently squeeze dry. Beat eggs with water; add salt. Arrange matzos in stacks of four. Dip in beaten egg and fry on both sides in a hot buttered skillet. Serve hot with jelly or honey. Serves 4 to 6.

MATZO KUGEL

3 matzos
6 eggs
1/2 cup sugar
1/2 teaspoon salt
1/4 teaspoon cinnamon
1/2 cup seedless raisins
1/2 cup chopped almonds
4 tart apples, shredded

grated rind of 1 orange
cinnamon–sugar mix (1/4
teaspoon cinnamon
and 1 tablespoon
sugar)
1/4 cup melted *schmaltz*
or butter

Crumble matzos into water and soak until soft; squeeze out all excess moisture. Beat eggs. Add sugar, salt, and cinnamon; continue beating until well blended. Stir crumbled matzos, raisins, almonds, apples, and orange rind into the egg mixture. Place in a well–greased 1 1/2–quart casserole. Sprinkle with cinnamon–sugar mix and pour melted *schmaltz* or butter over all. Bake at 350 degrees until firm and nicely browned (about 45 minutes). Serves 6 to 8.

MATZO KUGEL WITH GREBENES

5 matzos
1 onion, diced
1/4 cup *schmaltz*
1/4 cup chopped
  ***grebenes* (cracklings,**
  see page 48)

3 eggs
3 tablespoons sugar
1 teaspoon salt
pepper, to taste

Crumble matzos into water and soak until soft; squeeze out all excess moisture. Brown onion in *schmaltz*. Add onion, *schmaltz* and *grebenes* to crumbled matzos. Beat eggs well and add to them the sugar, salt, and pepper. Stir through the matzo mixture. Bake in a well–greased 1 1/2–quart casserole at 350 degrees until nicely browned (about 1 hour). Serves 6 to 8.

PASSOVER CARROT PUDDING*

1 cup matzo cake meal	1/2 cup brown sugar
1 teaspoon salt	1/2 cup kosher shortening
1 teaspoon cream of tartar	3 eggs, separated
1 teaspoon baking soda	3 cups grated raw carrots

Sift together dry ingredients. Cream sugar and shortening. Beat egg yolks until light. Alternately add egg yolks and dry ingredients to the creamed mixture; mix well. Stir in carrots. Fold in stiffly beaten egg whites. Bake in a well–greased aluminum mold or small tube pan 9 by 3 1/2 inches at 350 degrees for 40 minutes. Serve hot or cold. Serves 6 to 8.

* *Note:* This is not a dessert but a vegetable that can be served either with meat or dairy meals.

PASSOVER BLINTZES

1/2 cup potato flour	6 eggs
1/2 cup matzo cake meal	1 1/2 cups water
1/2 teaspoon salt	

Sift together potato flour, cake meal, and salt. Beat eggs until light. Add 1/2 cup water and beat again. Gradually add 1 cup water to the dry ingredients, stirring until smooth. Add beaten eggs to the batter, a small amount at a time, stirring each time until smooth.

Grease a 6–inch skillet lightly. Place over moderately high heat. Fill a cup with batter. When the skillet is hot, pour about 1/2 cup batter into the skillet. As soon as the batter clings to the bottom of the skillet (if your skillet is the right temperature, this will be almost immediately), pour the excess batter back into the cup. When the blintze "blisters" and the edges curl away from the sides of the skillet, invert the skillet over a wooden board and the blintze will fall out.

(It may be necessary to tap the edge of the skillet against the board.) The batter should be stirred again before frying each blintze. Grease the skillet about every third frying. It may take several blintzes before the skillet is "just right," and it may take several more before the cook gets the knack of making these paper–thin pancakes.

Place 1 tablespoon filling in the center of the cooked side of each blintze. Raise the bottom flap of dough to cover filling, then overlap with the top flap of dough. Tuck both sides under so that they almost meet at the bottom center. Another way of making blintzes is to place the filling near one edge and roll as you would a jelly roll. Brown lightly on both sides in a heavily greased skillet. Blintzes should be eaten hot. They may be served with sour cream, apple sauce, or both. Makes 22 to 24 blintzes.

BLINTZE FILLINGS

Cheese Filling

1 pound dry cottage cheese	2 tablespoons sour cream
	1/4 cup melted butter
2 eggs	1/2 teaspoon salt
1 tablespoon sugar (or to taste)	1 teaspoon lemon juice

Rub cottage cheese through a sieve and combine with remaining ingredients.

Meat Filling

2 cups leftover meat or boiled chicken	1 tablespoon *schmaltz*
	1 egg, beaten
1 onion, minced	salt and pepper, to taste

Put meat through a food grinder. Saute onion in *schmaltz* or shortening until golden. Combine all ingredients, including the fat in which the onion was sautéed. Additional seasonings may be added according to taste.

CAKE–MEAL BLINTZES

3 eggs   **1/2 teaspoon salt**
1 1/2 cups water   **3/4 cup matzo cake meal**

Beat eggs, add water, and beat again. Add salt. Place cake meal in a mixing bowl. Slowly add egg–water mixture, stirring constantly. If batter is lumpy, strain it, but do not add more water. Lightly grease a 6–inch skillet with a little fat. Place over a moderately high flame. Fill a cup with batter. Pour 1/2 cup of batter into the skillet. As soon as the batter adheres to the skillet, return excess batter to the cup.

Fry until blintze begins to "blister" and the edges curl away from the skillet. The blintze should be very thin and pliable and still very slightly moist on top. Turn out by inverting skillet over a wooden board. (It may be necessary to tap the edge of the skillet on the board.)

Batter should be stirred before each frying; grease skillet at about every third blintze. It may take several blintzes before the skillet is greased and heated just right. Fill and fry blintzes according to directions on page 110 and 111, using half the amount of filling called for. Makes 12.

MATZO–MEAL LATKES

[Pancakes]

1/2 cup matzo meal   **2 eggs, separated**
1/2 teaspoon salt   **1 cup milk or water**
1 tablespoon sugar

Mix together dry ingredients. Beat egg yolks with milk or water and add to matzo meal. Let stand 1 hour to swell.

Beat egg whites until stiff. Fold into matzo–meal batter. Pour from a tablespoon onto a well–greased, heated skillet. Brown on both sides. Serve hot with jelly, preserves, cinnamon–sugar mix, or sour cream. Serves 4 to 6.

CHEESE LATKES

(Pancakes)

1/2 pound dry cottage cheese	4 tablespoons matzo meal
6 eggs, separated	1/2 teaspoon salt

Rub cottage cheese through a sieve. Stir egg yolks into the cheese. Add matzo meal and salt. Mix well. Beat egg whites until stiff and fold into the cheese mixture. Drop from a tablespoon onto a hot buttered skillet. Fry on both sides until lightly browned. Serve hot with syrup, honey, or cinnamon–sugar mix. Serves 6.

STUFFED CHREMSLACH

6 eggs	2 1/2 tablespoons melted *schmaltz*
1 cup warm water	2 tablespoons potato starch
1 1/2 teaspoons salt	3 cups matzo meal
1/8 teaspoon pepper	
1/8 teaspoon ginger	

Beat eggs with water. Add seasonings and *schmaltz*; beat again. Sift potato starch and matzo meal together into the egg mixture. Mix well. This should make a fairly thick batter. Chill several hours or until firm enough to shape into patties. Wet the hands and shape the batter into flat patties of equal size (about 3 inches). Place a portion of stuffing on a patty and cover with another patty. Press the edges together and flatten chremslach slightly. Continue the process until all chremslach are stuffed. Fry in deep hot fat until golden brown and crisp on both sides. Makes 12 chremslach.

Stuffing

1 1/2 pound ground cooked meat	salt and pepper, to taste
1/2 onion, minced	1 tablespoon *schmaltz*

Combine all ingredients.

Note: Preserves may be used in place of meat stuffing.

POTATO KNAIDLECH

1 cup grated raw
   potatoes, well drained
1 cup mashed potatoes
2 eggs
1/2 cup matzo meal

2 tablespoons *schmaltz*
1/2 teaspoon salt
dash of pepper
1 tablespoon onion juice

Combine all ingredients and form into balls the size of a walnut. If not firm enough to shape, add more matzo meal. Drop into rapidly boiling salted water. Reduce heat and simmer slowly for 1 hour. Drain. Serve in chicken soup or with meat or chicken gravy. Serves 4 to 6.

PASSOVER MEAT LATKES

2 cups mashed potatoes
1/4 cup matzo cake meal
2 eggs, beaten
salt and pepper, to taste

1 cup ground leftover
   meat
schmaltz for frying

Combine first four ingredients and shape into 1 1/2 inch balls. Scoop a hole in the center of each ball and fill with ground meat. Press the potato mixture over the opening and flatten the balls slightly. Fry in a generous amount of hot *schmaltz* until lightly browned. Serves 4 to 6.

PASSOVER SPONGE CAKE

6 eggs, separated
juice of 1/2 lemon
1 cup sugar

1/4 cup potato flour
1/2 cup matzo cake meal

Beat yolks until thick and lemon colored. Stir in lemon juice. Beat egg whites until stiff but not dry. Gradually add sugar, 2 tablespoons at a time, beating after each addition. Beat until a stiff meringue is formed. Fold egg yolks into this mixture. Sift potato flour and cake meal together onto a piece of waxed paper. Sprinkle a small amount of the meal mixture on the egg mixture; fold in. Continue the process until all the meal is folded in. Bake in a small ungreased

tube pan (9 by 3 1/2 inches) at 325 degrees for 1 hour. Test
by sticking a clean broomstraw or toothpick deep into the
center of the cake. If it comes out clean, the cake is done.
Invert the pan until cool. Serves 10.

MATZO SPICE CAKE

12 eggs, separated
2 cups sugar
1 cup chopped almonds
1/3 cup Passover wine

1/4 teaspoon ground
cloves
1 1/2 teaspoon cinnamon
1 1/2 cups matzo cake
meal

Beat egg yolks with sugar until very light. Add nuts, wine,
spices, and cake meal. Mix well. Fold in stiffly beaten egg
whites. Bake in a large (10 by 4 inches) ungreased tube pan
at 325 degrees for about 1 hour. Test doneness by sticking
a clean broomstraw deep into the cake. If it comes out clean,
the cake is done. Invert until cool. Serves 12 to 14.

CHOCOLATE MATZO CAKE

8 eggs, separated
1 1/2 cups sugar
1/4 cup orange juice
**   or Passover wine**
1/2 cup grated nuts

1/3 cup potato starch
2/3 cup matzo cake meal
1/2 chocolate matzo,*
grated

Beat egg whites until stiff but not dry. Add sugar, 2 tablespoons at a time, continuing beating until a stiff meringue
is formed. Add juice or wine to egg yolk and beat until
thick. Fold egg yolks into meringue. Sift potato flour and
cake meal together onto a piece of waxed paper. Stir nuts
and grated chocolate into the meal mixture. Sprinkle a
small amount of the meal mixture onto the meringue; fold
in. Continue this process until all of the meal mixture has
been folded into the meringue. Bake in an ungreased small
tube pan (9 by 3 1/2 inches) at 325 degrees for 1 hour. Test
doneness by inserting a clean broomstraw or toothpick
deep into the cake. If it comes out clean, the cake is done.
Invert until cool. Serves 10.

* *Note:* Chocolate matzo is a candy sold during the Passover season. It may be procured at kosher delicatessens or butcher shops. One ounce sweet chocolate may be substituted by those who don't "keep pesach."

PASSOVER BANANA–NUT CAKE

9 eggs, separated
3/4 teaspoon salt
1 1/2 cups sifted sugar
2 very ripe bananas,
    mashed

1/2 cup chopped nuts
3/4 cup matzo cake meal
3/8 cup potato starch
juice of 1 lemon or
    juice of 1/2 orange

Beat egg whites with salt until a soft peak is formed. Gradually add sifted sugar, continuing beating until a stiff meringue is formed. Beat egg yolks; add bananas and nuts and beat well. Add egg yolk mixture to the stiffly beaten whites. Beat. Sift cake meal and potato starch together three times. Gradually add the meal mixture to the egg mixture, continuing beating. Add lemon juice or orange juice. Beat again. Add 1 tablespoon cold water and beat until well blended. Pour into a 10–inch tube pan that has been lined with brown paper. Bake at 350 degrees for 1 hour. Test with a straw or toothpick (see page 115) or by pressing a fingertip against the cake; if it leaves no dent, the cake is done. Invert until cool. Serves 12.

PASSOVER DATE TORTE

8 eggs, separated
1 7/8 cups sugar
juice and grated rind of
    1 lemon and 1 orange
1 1/3 cups matzo meal
2 tablespoons unsweet–
    ened cocoa

1/4 teaspoon ground
    allspice
25 dates, diced
1/4 teaspoon ground
    cloves
1/2 cup chopped nuts
    (walnuts or pecans)
1 apple, grated

Beat egg yolks with sugar. Stir in lemon and orange juice and grated rinds. Sift dry ingredients into the batter; mix well. Stir in dates, nuts, and apple. Fold in stiffly beaten egg whites. Bake in an ungreased 9–inch spring form, lined with waxed paper, at 350 degrees for about 1 1/4 hours. Test as on page 115. Serves 14.

PASSOVER INGBERLECH

2 eggs	1 1/2 tablespoons ginger
1 cup sugar	1 cup matzo meal
3/4 cup honey	sugar and ginger to
1/2 cup chopped	sprinkle over top
almonds	

Beat eggs until light. Combine sugar and honey and bring to a boil in a deep saucepan. Cook 10 minutes and remove from heat. Add remaining ingredients to the eggs; mix well, using a fork. Add to syrup. Cook over low heat, stirring constantly, until brown and almost too thick to stir, or until a candy thermometer registers the "soft crack" stage. Turn out on a wet board. Dip hands in ice water; using the palms of the hands, flatten the mixture to 1/2–inch thickness. Sprinkle with sugar and ginger and let cool slightly. Cut with a sharp wet knife into squares or diamonds. Makes about 25.

FARFEL CANDY

1 pound honey	3/4 cup matzo farfel
1/4 cup sugar	3 cups chopped nuts

Boil honey and sugar on a low flame until brown or until a candy thermometer registers the soft crack stage (about 20 minutes). Stir in farfel and nuts. Turn out on a wet board. Wet the hands with ice water and pat the candy into a square 3/4 inch thick. Let cool slightly. Cut with a sharp, wet knife into squares or diamonds. Makes about 50.

NUENT (NUT CANDY)

1 pint honey
1/2 cup sugar

1 1/2 pounds nuts
    (walnuts or pecans),
    finely chopped

Bring honey and sugar to a boil; boil for 10 minutes. Slowly add nuts. Cook until thick or until a candy thermometer registers the "soft crack" stage. Spoon out onto a wet wooden board. Dip hands in ice water and cut into a square 1 inch thick. Let cool slightly. Cut into squares or diamonds, using a sharp wet knife.

❤ 16 ❤

YOM KIPPUR COOKERY

Ah ha! You looked. Shame on you! You should be fasting.

BAGELS WITHOUT LOX

About bagels with or without lox I've got nothing to say. You think it's easy to write a book?

BAGELS

8 cups flour	1/4 cup salad oil
1 tablespoon salt	4 eggs, slightly beaten
1 tablespoon sugar	2 tablespoons sugar
2 cakes fresh yeast	2 quarts boiling water
2 cups lukewarm potato water *	poppy seed or sesame seed (optional)

Sift together dry ingredients into a large mixing bowl.

Soften yeast in one third of the potato water. Add to the flour. Add oil to the remaining potato water and stir into the flour mixture. Add eggs and stir briskly to form a ball of dough.

Knead on a lightly floured board for 10 minutes. This must be a firm dough; add more flour if necessary. Return to the bowl, smooth side up. Cover with a tea towel and let rise at room temperature until the dough rises to the top of the bowl. Knead again on a lightly floured board until smooth and elastic (as for rolls). Pinch off pieces of dough and roll them between the palms to form ropes about 6 inches long and 3/4 inch wide. Pinch the ends together firmly to make a doughnut shape.

Add sugar to boiling water. Drop bagels into the water one at a time. As they come to the surface, turn them over. Boil 1 minute longer on the second side. Place on a greased cookie sheet and bake at 450 degrees until the crust is golden brown and crisp (10 to 15 minutes). Bagels may be sprinkled with poppy seed or sesame seed before baking, if desired. Makes about 30.

* *Note:* Potato water is water in which peeled potatoes have cooked. Plain water may be used, but it is not as good.

CHALLAH

(Sabbath bread)

1 cake fresh yeast	**1 tablespoon sugar**
1/4 cup warm water	**1 tablespoon salad oil**
5 cups flour	**1 egg, beaten**
1 teaspoon salt	**warm water**

GLAZE:
  1 egg yolk diluted with 1 teaspoon water
  poppy seed or sesame seed (optional)

Soften yeast in 1/4 cup warm water. Sift together dry ingredients. Add oil. Add softened yeast and beaten egg.

Mix thoroughly, adding just enough water for smooth kneading. Knead well. Place in a bowl and cover with a tea towel. Let stand until it "bubbles." Knead again. Cover; let rise until doubled in bulk.

Divide dough into three equal parts. Roll into three strips and braid them. Place in a baking pan and let rise until doubled in bulk.

Just before baking, brush with diluted egg yolk. Sprinkle with poppy seed or sesame seed if desired. Bake at 350 degrees until golden brown (about 1 hour).

ALMOND BREAD

3 eggs
1/2 cup sugar
1 1/2 cups sifted flour

2 teaspoons baking powder
1/2 cup finely chopped almonds

Beat eggs. Add sugar gradually and continue beating until creamy. Sift together flour and baking powder. Add almonds and mix well. Add flour mixture to egg mixture; stir until smooth. Pour into a well–greased loaf pan 10 1/4 by 3 5/8 by 2 5/8 inches. Bake for 1 hour at 350 degrees. Serves 8.

CHEESE ROLLS

2 cups flour
1/4 cup sugar
2 teaspoons baking powder
1/2 teaspoon salt

1 egg, separated
1 cup milk
1/2 cup grated American cheese

Sift together dry ingredients. Add beaten egg yolk and milk. Beat for 1 minute. Fold in cheese and stiffly beaten egg white. Bake in greased muffin tins at 400 degrees for about 20 minutes. Makes 12 rolls.

❤ 18 ❤

You Can Be Normal, Too, Why Not?

Nowadays everything is psychology. You want to go in business, you need psychology. You want to have children, you need psychology. And everybody has complexes—a new word. In my day, we didn't know from complexes. People were either *verrucked, zudreht, vermished,* or *meshuga*—that is to say, they were either not all there, confused, mixed up, or just plain crazy. Nowadays every intelligent person has complexes and they're running like crazy to psychiatrists. If you ask me, no one in his right mind would go to one.

Nowadays, people are either normal or not normal. Take me, for instance, I'm normal and it's so easy to be normal that I can't understand why people should be not normal. If you know how to read and you got eyes and ears for television, then there is no reason why you shouldn't be normal. Every day there are experts telling you what is normal and how to be it.

One day I am listening to television with my daughter. It is just before we are moving to our new one–floor–plan ranch–type house. The lady on television is telling that some children are not adjusted to moving. They don't want to move ... so do them something. Crazy, yes? So what does she say? She says if you've got children like this, so promise them a nice present or let them take with them old, familiar objects.

"Mama," cries my little darling, "buy me a new bicycle, I'm unjusted to moving."

"Darling, mine," I'm saying, "Mama saw the same program. So take with you all the *alte schmates* (old rags) like your mother is taking with her the old furniture, and you'll be 'justed'." It's that simple.

Now it's writing in our newspaper every day a woman psychologist. You're writing to her letters and she's telling you in the newspaper what complexes you got and what is normal.

"A normal woman," she says, "is outgoing." You think maybe she means is going out? Never. The outgoing woman is staying in and being outgoing. And while she is staying in and being outgoing, it's coming in to her friends.

So if this is normal, so I can be normal, too. So all the time I'm staying in and being outgoing it's coming in to me friends. Friends? A regular army. In the morning, at noon, at night. I'm making from my house a regular hotel.

Nu, so what can you do? When people are coming into the house, you can't let them go hungry, no? But eight–course meals I'm not serving them. That normal I'm not. To be that normal you have to be a little crazy.

So I'm having in the house always a little something—a glass tea with lemon, a piece fruit, a coffee cake. From this you can't starve, no?

So don't worry. You can be normal, too; for this you don't need to go to college. Here are the recipes you should have always in the house a little something.

COTTAGE CHEESE CHEESECAKE

1 pound dry cottage
    cheese
4 tablespoons cornstarch
6 eggs, separated
1 pint sour cream
1 cup sugar

1 teaspoon lemon juice
1 teaspoon grated lemon
    rind
1 teaspoon vanilla
16 graham crackers

Rub cottage cheese through a sieve. Stir in cornstarch. Beat in egg yolks, one at a time. Stir in sour cream. Add 2/3 cup sugar, lemon juice, lemon rind, and vanilla.

Beat egg whites until stiff but not dry. Gradually add 1/3 cup sugar and continue beating until a stiff meringue is formed. Fold egg whites into cheese mixture.

Crush graham crackers finely. Spread evenly on the bottom of a 9–inch spring form pan. Pour in cheese mixture.

Bake at 350 degrees for 1 hour. Turn off heat, open oven door, and let cake remain in the oven until cool. Serves 10.

CREAM CHEESE CHEESECAKE

16 graham crackers, finely crushed	2 eggs
1/2 cup melted butter	1/2 cup sugar
12 ounces cream cheese	1 teaspoon vanilla
	1 pint sour cream

Mix crushed graham crackers with melted butter; pat into the bottom of a 9–inch spring form. Beat cream cheese and eggs until smooth and well–blended. Pour into graham–cracker crust. Bake for 20 minutes in a 350 degree oven. Cool completely (at least 1 hour). Add sugar and vanilla to sour cream. Spread over cooled cheesecake and bake for 5 minutes at 375 degrees. Cool and refrigerate. Serves 10.

PINEAPPLE CHEESECAKE

Crust

12 graham crackers, finely crushed	2 tablespoons sugar
	1/4 pound butter, melted

Filling

9 ounces cream cheese	1/2 teaspoon vanilla
2 eggs	2 1/2 cups crushed pineapple, drained
1/2 cup sugar	

Topping

1 pint sour cream	1 teaspoon vanilla
3 tablespoons sugar	

Mix the finely crushed graham crackers with sugar and melted butter. Press into the bottom of a small spring form pan or 8–inch square cake pan.

To make the filling, combine cream cheese, eggs, sugar, and vanilla. Blend until smooth. Add drained crushed pineapple and blend well. Pour cream cheese mixture over the crust and bake at 375 degrees for 20 minutes. Let cool for 1 hour.

Mix sour cream, sugar, and vanilla and spread mixture over the cake. Return to a 375 degree oven and bake for 5 minutes. Cool and chill. Serves 10.

CHEESE PIE

Crust

4 tablespoons shortening
2 egg yolks, beaten with
   3 tablespoons water
1 teaspoon lemon juice

1/2 cup sifted flour
1 teaspoon baking powder
1/2 teaspoon salt
2 tablespoons sugar

Cream shortening. Add egg yolks beaten with water. Add lemon juice and blend. Sift together dry ingredients. Add to creamed mixture and mix until smooth. Spoon mixture into a large (10–inch) pie pan, spreading over the sides and bottom.

Filling

1 1/2 cups dry cottage
   cheese
2 tablespoons sifted
   flour
1/4 teaspoon salt
2 tablespoons cream
3 eggs, separated
3/4 cup sugar

1 tablespoon melted
   butter
1 teaspoon lemon juice
1 1/2 teaspoons grated
   lemon rind
1/4 pound almonds,
   chopped

Rub cottage cheese through a sieve. Mix with flour, salt, and cream. Beat egg yolks. Gradually add 1/2 cup sugar to yolks and continue beating until smooth and thick. Stir melted butter, lemon juice, and rind into the egg mixture, then add it to the cottage cheese mixture. Beat egg whites until stiff but not dry. Gradually add 1/4 cup sugar and continue beating to form a stiff meringue. Fold into the cottage–cheese mixture. Pour into the pie crust and sprinkle with chopped almonds. Bake at 325 degrees until firm (about 1 1/4 hours). Serve cold. Serves 10.

CREAM CHEESE PIE

Crust

4 tablespoons butter
3 tablespoons sugar
1 egg, beaten

1 cup sifted flour
1/2 teaspoon baking powder

Cream butter and sugar until light; add beaten egg. Sift together flour and baking powder. Add to the creamed mixture and stir until smooth. Pat firmly into a 10–inch greased pie pan, covering the sides and bottom.

Filling

1/2 pound cream cheese
2 eggs, well beaten
3 tablespoons sugar
2 tablespoons flour

2 cups milk
1/2 teaspoon vanilla
juice of 1 lemon

Mash cream cheese with a fork until soft. Add eggs, sugar, and flour; blend well. Add milk, vanilla, and lemon juice; stir until smooth. Pour into unbaked pie shell and bake at 325 degrees until firm (about 1 1/2 hours). Chill. Serves 10.

HUNGARIAN COFFEE CRESCENT

1/2 pound butter
1 cake fresh yeast
3 egg yolks
1/2 cup sugar

1 teaspoon salt
1 cup cold milk
4 1/2 cups unsifted flour

Allow the butter to soften at room temperature. Crumble yeast into butter and cream them together. Add egg yolks and sugar, continuing creaming. Add salt and cold milk. Sift in flour and knead in the bowl until the dough leaves the sides of the bowl.

Remove dough from the bowl, butter the bowl, and return the dough to the bowl. Cover with a tea towel and set in a warm place until the dough has doubled in bulk. Divide the dough in half. Keep one part in the covered bowl and use to make Hungarian Kuchen (see page 131). Roll the second half to 1/4-inch thickness and fill as follows.

Filling

3 egg whites
3 tablespoons melted
    butter
1/2 cup coarsely chop-
    ped nuts

1 teaspoon cinnamon
    mixed with 4 table-
    spoons sugar
sugar for glaze

Reserve a small part of egg white for the glaze; beat the remaining whites until stiff. Spread the dough with melted butter, then with stiffly beaten egg whites. Sprinkle with nuts and cinnamon-sugar mix. Roll as a jelly roll and press ends together to seal.

Place in a 9-inch layer-cake pan and shape into the form of a crescent. Place an inverted custard cup at the center of the crescent so that the cake will retain its crescent shape while rising and baking. Let rise until doubled in bulk. Brush with remaining egg white and sprinkle with sugar. Bake at 375 degrees for about 45 minutes. Serves about 10.

HUNGARIAN KUCHEN

Use half of the dough from the preceding Coffee Crescent recipe. Press the dough into an 8-inch square cake pan and let rise until doubled in bulk.

Cover with Streusel Topping and bake at 375 degrees for about 45 minutes. Serves about 10.

Streusel Topping

1/2 cup brown sugar,
    firmly packed
4 tablespoons flour
1 1/2 teaspoons cinnamon

1/2 cup chopped nuts
3 tablespoons melted
    butter

Blend all ingredients to the consistency of coarse crumbs. Sprinkle over top of kuchen before baking.

BUTTER KUCHEN OR SCHNECKEN

1 cake fresh yeast	2 eggs, beaten
2 tablespoons lukewarm water	1 cup milk
4 cups flour	1/3 cup sugar
1/4 teaspoon salt	1/3 cup butter

Soften yeast in lukewarm water. Sift together flour and salt. Make a depression in the center of the flour and put in softened yeast and beaten eggs. Let stand. Scald (do not boil) milk, sugar, and butter. Let stand until lukewarm and add to the flour.

Beat thoroughly until air bubbles form. This mixture should have the consistency of a soft biscuit dough. If necessary, add a little more flour.

Cover the bowl with a tea towel and let stand until the dough has doubled in bulk.

This is the dough for both Kuchen and Schnecken.

KUCHEN

2 teaspoons cinnamon mixed with 1/2 cup sugar	melted butter

Divide dough in four parts. Knead each part on a lightly floured board. Press one part into the bottom of an 8–inch square cake pan. Spread with melted butter and sprinkle with cinnamon–sugar mix. Cover with an equal amount of dough, and again brush with melted butter and sprinkle with cinnamon–sugar mix.

Bake at 350 degrees for about 45 minutes. Makes two kuchen. A kuchen serves 6 people or 1 teenage boy.

SCHNECKEN

1/4 pound butter, melted
chopped nuts
raisins

cinnamon–sugar mix
(see above)
brown sugar

Divide dough in four parts. Roll out dough, one part at a time, to 1/8–inch thickness on a lightly floured board. Brush each piece with melted butter. Sprinkle with nuts, raisins, and cinnamon–sugar mix. Roll up as a jelly roll and cut into 1 1/4–inch pieces.

Put the pieces in large muffin tins that have been buttered and sugared, using 1/4 teaspoon melted butter and 1/4 teaspoon brown sugar for each muffin cup. Let rise until the dough fills the muffin cup.

Bake at 350 degrees for about 25 minutes. Makes about 30.

SOUR CREAM COFFEE CAKE

1 cup sugar
1/4 pound butter
2 eggs
1/2 pint sour cream

2 cups sifted cake flour
1 teaspoon baking powder
1 teaspoon baking soda
1 teaspoon vanilla

Topping

1/4 cup sugar
1/2 teaspoon cinnamon

1/2 cup chopped nuts

Cream butter and sugar. Add eggs and sour cream; beat until smooth. Sift together dry ingredients and add to egg mixture. Add vanilla; blend thoroughly.

Pour half of the batter into a small greased tube pan (9 by 3 1/2 inches). Sprinkle with half of the topping mixture.

Add the remaining batter and sprinkle with the remainder of the topping mixture. Bake at 350 degrees for 35 minutes. Serves 6 to 8.

BABKE (BATTER COFFEE CAKE)

1 cake fresh yeast	1/2 cup butter
1 cup warm milk	3 eggs, beaten
1/4 teaspoon salt	1/2 cup raisins
3/4 cup sugar	1 tablespoon grated
3 3/4 cups flour	lemon rind

Soften yeast in a small amount of the warm milk in a small mixing bowl. Add remainder of milk, salt, 1 teaspoon sugar, and 1 cup flour to the softened yeast. Beat well and let rise.

When the yeast mixture has risen to at least one and one–half times its original size and is "spongy," cream the butter with the remaining sugar. Add the beaten eggs and the yeast mixture. Beat thoroughly.

Add raisins, lemon rind, and the remainder of the flour. Mix until smooth; this should make a thick batter. Let rise until doubled in bulk.

Divide the batter in half, and place each half in a well–greased 8–inch square cake pan. Let rise again until at least doubled in bulk.

When the cakes have risen sufficiently, brush with melted butter and sprinkle with Streusel Topping (see page 131). Bake at 375 degrees until lightly browned (about 45 minutes). Each coffee cake serves 8 to 10.

HUNGARIAN ALMOND TORTE

1/2 pound butter	1/4 pound ground almonds
1/2 cup powdered sugar	2 cups flour

Filling

1 pound English walnuts,	scant 1/2 cup sweet cream
ground	1 cup whipping cream
1 cup powdered sugar	

Cream butter and sugar. Add almonds. Work in flour with the fingertips until the mixture is completely blended. Divide the dough into four parts. Pat each portion into the bottom of an 8–inch layer cake pan.

Bake in a moderate oven, 350 degrees, until lightly browned (about 15 minutes). Cool and remove from pans.

Make a paste of the ground walnuts, powdered sugar, and just enough sweet cream to moisten. Divide the filling into three equal parts. Spread three layers with nut paste. Stack the layers, topping them with a plain layer.

One hour before serving, cover top and sides of torte with whipped cream. Refrigerate until ready to serve. Serves 8 to 10.

CINNAMON–NUT ROLLS

1 cake fresh yeast
1/4 cup warm milk
1/2 pound butter
4 tablespoons sugar
2 eggs

2 cups flour
cinnamon–sugar mix (2 teaspoons cinnamon and 1/2 cup sugar)
chopped nuts

Soften yeast in warm milk. Cream together butter and sugar until smooth. Beat in eggs one at a time. Alternately stir in flour and softened yeast. Cover with waxed paper and refrigerate overnight.

Divide dough in half and roll out, one part at a time, to 1/4–inch thickness on a board that has been sprinkled with cinnamon–sugar mix.

Sprinkle each half with cinnamon–sugar mix and chopped nuts. Roll up as a jelly roll. Cut in 1 1/2–inch slices and place cut side down on a baking tin. Bake at 350 degrees until lightly browned (about 20 minutes). Serves 6.

CARROT ROLLS

1 cake fresh yeast	pinch of salt
1/4 cup lukewarm water	1 egg, beaten
1 cup milk	3 cups unsifted flour
1/4 pound butter	flour for kneading
1/2 cup sugar	

Filling
2 cups grated raw carrots   3/4 cup honey
1/2 cup seedless raisins

Topping
honey   poppy seed

Soften yeast in lukewarm water. Scald milk, and to it add butter, sugar, and salt. Cool to lukewarm and stir in beaten egg. Stir in yeast mixture. Transfer to a mixing bowl. Add unsifted flour 1 cup at a time, stirring until smooth after each addition. Cover the bowl with a tea towel. Refrigerate overnight or longer. (This will keep for a week.) This makes a batter so thin you will think you made an error in mixing. Don't despair; extra flour will be added when kneaded.

When ready to make rolls, prepare the filling by cooking carrots and raisins in boiling honey until the carrots are tender. Set aside to cool. Spoon batter onto a *heavily* floured board. Knead for 5 minutes. If necessary, add more flour until the dough is stiff enough to roll out. Roll dough to 1/4–inch thickness.

Spread with carrot–raisin mixture and roll up as a jelly roll. Slice at 1 1/2 inch intervals. Place 2 inches apart on baking tins, uncut sides down, and let rise until doubled in size. Bake at 350 degrees for 10 minutes. Remove from the oven, brush with honey, and sprinkle with poppy seed. Return to the oven and bake until golden brown (about 10 minutes more). Serves 8.

LEKACH (HONEY CAKE)

4 eggs
1 cup sugar
1 cup honey
1/2 cup strong black
    coffee
2 tablespoons salad oil
3 1/2 cups flour
1 1/2 teaspoons baking
    powder
1 teaspoon baking soda

1/4 teaspoon ground
    cloves
1/2 teaspoon ground
    allspice
1/2 teaspoon cinnamon
1/2 cup chopped nuts
1/2 cup raisins
1/4 cup citron, finely cut
2 tablespoons brandy

Beat eggs. Add sugar gradually, beating until creamy. Combine honey and coffee. Stir into oil. Combine with egg mixture. Sift together flour, baking powder, soda, and spices. Add nuts, raisins, and citron to flour mixture. Add egg mixture to dry ingredients. Blend thoroughly. Stir brandy through the batter. Line two greased loaf pans (10 1/4 by 3 5/8 by 2 5/8) with waxed paper. Half fill each pan with batter. Bake at 300 degrees for 1 1/4 hours. Each cake serves 8.

HONEY CAKE

2 eggs, separated
1 cup sugar
3/4 cup honey
3 cups flour
1 teaspoon baking
    powder

1 teaspoon baking soda
1/2 teaspoon cinnamon
1/2 teaspoon ground
    allspice
1 cup black coffee
1/2 cup chopped nuts

Combine egg yolks, sugar, and honey; beat well. Sift together flour, baking powder, soda, and spices. Alternately add flour mixture and coffee to honey mixture. Mix well. Stir in nuts. Fold in stiffly beaten egg whites. Pour into an 8–inch square cake pan that has been greased and lined with waxed paper. Bake at 350 degrees for 1 hour. Serves 10 to 12.

HONEY–RAISIN CAKE

1 cup seedless raisins
3 cups flour, unsifted
1 teaspoon baking
  powder
1 teaspoon salt
1/2 teaspoon ground
  cloves
1/2 teaspoon ground
  allspice
1 teaspoon ground
  nutmeg

1 teaspoon cinnamon
1 ounce bitter chocolate
1 teaspoon baking soda
1/2 cup shortening
1 cup sugar
1/2 cup honey
4 eggs
1 teaspoon vanilla
1 teaspoon lemon extract
1/2 cup grated pecans

Boil raisins in 2 cups water for 10 minutes. While raisins are boiling, sift together flour, baking powder, salt, and spices two times. Remove raisins from the heat and add bitter chocolate to raisins and raisin liquid. When the chocolate has melted, strain and set the raisins aside. Add baking soda to the strained liquid while it is still warm.

Cream together shortening and sugar. Add honey; blend well. Add eggs one at a time, beating after each addition. Add vanilla and lemon extract. Alternately add flour mixture and raisin liquid to the creamed mixture, mixing well after each addition. Add raisins and grated nuts; mix well. Put in two loaf pans (10 1/4 by 3 5/8 by 2 5/8 inches) that have been greased and lined with waxed paper. Bake at 375 degrees for 50 minutes. Each cake serves about 8.

SPONGE CAKE

6 eggs, separated
1 1/2 cups sugar
1/2 cup water

1 1/2 cups sifted flour
1 teaspoon vanilla or
  almond extract

Beat egg whites until stiff. Gradually add sugar and continue beating until stiff meringue is formed. Beat egg yolks, adding water gradually, and continue beating until yolks are light. Fold one third of the egg yolks into whites, then one third of flour. Continue in this way until all yolks and flour have been used. Stir in flavoring. Turn into a tubed spring form and bake at 350 degrees for about 45 minutes. Serves 6.

APPLESAUCE HONEY CAKE

1 pound honey	1 teaspoon baking soda
3 eggs	1/2 teaspoon cinnamon
1 1/2 cups sugar	1/4 teaspoon nutmeg
2 cups applesauce	1 cup diced crystallized
4 cups flour	fruit

Beat together honey and eggs. Add sugar and applesauce; beat well. Add flour, which has been sifted with soda and spices. Stir in fruit. Grease two loaf pans (10 1/4 by 3 5/8 by 2 5/8 inches) or one 8–inch square cake pan and line with waxed paper. Put in batter and bake at 350 degrees for 1 hour. Serves about 16.

TAYGLECH

4 eggs	1/2 pound pecans,
3 tablespoons oil	quartered
2 1/2 cups flour	1 tablespoon ground
1 teaspoon baking	ginger (or more)
powder	2 tablespoons Bourbon
1 pound honey	whisky or water
3/4 cup sugar	

Beat together eggs and oil. Sift together flour and baking powder. Add to the egg mixture and knead in the bowl until smooth. Pinch off pieces of dough and roll between the hands to form ropes 1/2 inch or less in diameter. Cut ropes into 1/2–inch pieces.

Bring honey and sugar to a rapid boil in a Dutch oven or any heavy, broad–bottomed pan with a tight cover. Drop dough into boiling honey a few pieces at a time (so that the temperature will not fall below the boiling point). Cover and boil for 5 minutes. Remove from heat, stir, and cover. Place in a 375–degree oven for 30 to 45 minutes, removing to stir at 15–minute intervals. After tayglech have been in the oven for 30 minutes, remove one and test by breaking it open with a fork. If it is not crisp, return to the oven for another 15–minute period. If crisp, stir in nuts and ginger. Cover and return to the oven for 5 minutes. Remove from the oven and sprinkle with Bourbon or water.

Turn out on a wet wooden board. Using a wet rolling pin, gently spread tayglech into a large square. When cool, cut into squares or diamonds of the desired size, using a sharp, wet knife. Tayglech will keep for a very long time if stored in tightly covered containers. This recipe makes enough tayglech for company, but not enough for a bar mitzvah.

Note: Do not make tayglech in hot, humid weather because the honey will remain sticky; but then, who wants to go to so much trouble in such weather?

COOKED TAYGLECH

1/2 cup oil	1/8 teaspoon ginger
8 eggs, beaten	2 pounds honey
4 1/2 cups flour (scant)	1 pound brown sugar
2 teaspoons baking powder	2 teaspoons ginger
1/8 teaspoon cinnamon	1 cup walnuts, broken into coarse pieces

Stir oil into beaten eggs. Sift together flour, baking powder, cinnamon, and 1/8 teaspoon ginger. Add flour mixture to the egg–oil mixture. Knead thoroughly. This should make a dough that is soft yet firm enough to roll. Pinch off pieces of dough and roll between the hands to form ropes about 1/2 inch thick. Cut ropes at 1/2–inch intervals. Place these 1/2 inch pieces of dough on a floured cookie sheet. Bake in a 350–degree oven until lightly browned (about 20 minutes).

Place honey, brown sugar, and 2 teaspoons ginger in a large deep kettle and bring to a rapid boil. Drop browned tayglech into the honey mixture, stirring constantly with a wooden spoon. When tayglech begin to turn reddish brown, drop in walnuts. Continue to stir for about 30 minutes. Test by dropping one "taygle" into cold water; it is done when the honey forms a hard crust on the outside. Turn out onto a wet wooden board and let cool just a few minutes. Dip the hands in ice water and form into 2–inch balls.

DRY TAYGLECH

1/2 cup oil	1/8 teaspoon ginger
8 eggs, beaten	1 cup walnut halves
4 1/2 cups flour (scant)	1 1/2 cups white sugar
2 teaspoons baking	2 cups brown sugar
powder	1 tablespoon ginger
1/8 teaspoon cinnamon	

Prepare dough and roll out in ropes as in the preceding recipe. Wind a rope of dough around a walnut half so that the nut is completely covered. Continue this process until all the dough has been used. Place these dough balls on a floured cookie sheet. Bake in a 350–degree oven until lightly browned (about 20 minutes). Remove from oven.

Place white sugar, brown sugar, and 1 tablespoon ginger in a deep saucepan. Cook over a very low flame, stirring constantly with a wooden spoon, until all the sugars are melted. Drop Tayglech into the syrup and stir constantly (to prevent sticking) until all the sugar has crystallized around them. Remove to a platter. These tayglech are perfectly dry when done.

ALMOND COOKIES

2 cups ground almonds	1/2 cup sugar
1/2 cup melted butter	powdered sugar
(scant)	

Add sugar to ground almonds. Add only enough melted butter to hold them together. Place on waxed paper and pat into a very thin layer. Cut into small rounds with a biscuit cutter. Place on an ungreased cookie sheet and bake at 350 degrees until lightly browned (about 12 minutes). Dust with powdered sugar.

ALMOND MACAROONS

1/2 pound blanched almonds
4 egg whites

2 cups confectioners sugar, sifted

Pound almonds to a paste and mix with sugar. Beat egg whites until stiff; fold into the almond–sugar mixture. Wet the hands with cold water and roll paste into balls the size of a walnut. Place 1 inch apart on baking tins that have been covered with waxed paper. Bake at 325 degrees until lightly browned (about 45 minutes).

SOUR CREAM ALMOND COOKIES

3 eggs
1 cup sugar
1 teaspoon vanilla
1 cup sour cream
4 cups sifted flour

4 teaspoons baking powder
1 cup almonds, finely chopped
granulated sugar

Beat eggs. Add sugar gradually, continuing beating until creamy. Stir in vanilla and sour cream. Sift together flour and baking powder. Add nuts and mix well. Add dry ingredients to the egg mixture, mixing thoroughly. Roll dough to 1/8–inch thickness and sprinkle with sugar. Cut with a cookie cutter. Bake at 425 degrees for 15 minutes.

MANDELBROT

4 cups flour
1 teaspoon baking powder
pinch of salt
1 cup sugar

4 eggs
1/2 cup salad oil
1 teaspoon vanilla
1 cup cut almonds, each nut cut in thirds

Sift flour, baking powder, and salt into a bowl. Put sugar in another bowl and beat in eggs one at a time. Add oil and vanilla. Alternately add flour and almonds to egg mixture, mixing thoroughly. Knead well on a lightly floured board.

Divide dough into eight rolls about 1 inch high and 2 inches wide. Bake on greased cookie sheets in a 350–degree oven for 20 minutes. Remove from the oven. Slice each roll at 1–inch intervals. Place slices, cut side down, on cookie sheets. Return to the oven and bake at 275 degrees for 20 minutes on each side or until lightly browned and crisp.

HAMENTASCHEN

2 cups sifted flour	pinch of salt
1 1/2 teaspoons baking powder	2 eggs, beaten
6 tablespoons sugar	3 tablespoons salad oil

Sift together dry ingredients. Make a depression in the center and add eggs and oil. Mix thoroughly. Roll dough out to 1/8–inch thickness on a lightly floured board. Cut into rounds about 3 inches in diameter. Place a tablespoon of filling (see page 145) on each round. Bring three sides of the circles together at the center to form triangles. Pinch the edges together to form a slight ridge. Bake on a greased baking tin in a 350–degree oven until golden brown (about 30 minutes). Makes 12 small Hamentaschen.

YEAST HAMENTASCHEN

2 cakes fresh yeast	1 cup water, or water in which peeled potatoes have been cooked
1/4 cup lukewarm water	
1 1/2 teaspoons salt	
1/2 cup sugar	5 cups sifted flour (about)
1/2 cup melted shorten- ing	3 eggs, beaten
	egg yolk for glaze

Soften yeast in lukewarm water. Add salt, sugar, and shortening to water or potato water. Add 2 cups flour; beat thoroughly. Add yeast and eggs, mixing well. Add the remaining flour to make a soft dough. Knead on a lightly floured board until shiny. Place in a lightly greased bowl, cover with a tea towel, and let stand in a warm place until the dough has doubled in bulk. Punch down the dough and turn it over. Cover with a tea towel. Chill in the refrigerator overnight.

Divide the dough into balls the size of a small apple. Roll out to rounds 1/4 inch thick. Place a tablespoon of filling (see recipes which follow) in the center of each round. Bring three sides of the circle together at the center to form a triangle. Pinch edges together to form a slight ridge. Let stand at room temperature until doubled in bulk. Brush tops with an egg yolk diluted with 1 tablespoon water. Place very far apart on greased baking tins and bake at 350 degrees until golden brown (about 35 minutes). Makes 15 very large Hamentaschen.

COOKIE-DOUGH HAMENTASCHEN

1 cup sugar	**6 tablespoons water**
1 1/3 cups shortening	**1/2 teaspoon vanilla**
2 eggs	**4 cups sifted flour**

Cream together sugar and shortening. Add eggs and continue creaming until smooth. Stir in water and vanilla. Add sifted flour, mixing until the dough forms a ball. Wrap in waxed paper and refrigerate overnight.

Pinch off pieces of dough to form balls the size of a very small apple. Roll out or pat out each piece on waxed paper to form a circle 1/4 inch thick. Place a portion of filling (see below) in the center of each round.

Bring three sides of the circle together at the center to form a triangle. Pinch the edges together to form a slight seam or ridge.

Bake on a greased baking tin at 375 degrees until golden brown (about 15 minutes). Makes 24.

HAMENTASCH FILLINGS

Prune

1 pound prunes, stewed
1 cup chopped nuts
1 tablespoon lemon juice

1/4 teaspoon cinnamon
mixed with 1 table–
spoon sugar

Remove pits from prunes. Chop prunes and nuts very fine. Add lemon juice and cinnamon–sugar mix.

Povidla

1 pound prunes
1 cup raisins
1/2 cup nuts

1/2 orange (pulp and rind)
1/4 cup sugar

Cook prunes and remove pits. Pour boiling water over raisins and let stand until plump. Drain. Put prunes, raisins, nuts, and orange through the medium blade of a food chopper. Add sugar.

Poppy Seed

1 cup poppy seed
boiling water
2 tablespoons sugar
1/4 cup honey

pinch of salt
1/2 cup water
1/2 cup finely chopped
almonds

Pour boiling water over poppy seed and let stand until cool; drain. Pound seeds well. (If they are large, they can be run through a food grinder.) Cook together poppy seed, sugar, honey, salt, and water over moderate heat until thick, stirring frequently. Remove from heat and stir in chopped almonds. Cool.

Cheese

8 ounces dry cottage
  cheese
3 ounces cream cheese
2 eggs, well beaten

1/3 cup sugar
2 tablespoons cracker
  meal
1/2 teaspoon cinnamon

Rub cottage cheese through a sieve. Cream together cottage cheese and cream cheese, using a fork. Combine all ingredients and mix well.

CARROT PIROSKI

2 cups flour (or more)
pinch of salt
1 ounce poppy seed

6 eggs, slightly beaten
3/4 cup oil

Combine all ingredients. Knead until the dough holds its shape, adding more flour if necessary. Roll out very thin and cut into 2–inch squares.

FILLING

2 1/2 pounds carrots,
  grated
3 cups sugar

1/2 teaspoon ginger
1 pint honey

Place carrots, sugar, and 1/4 cup water in an uncovered saucepan and boil until the mixture holds its shape. Add ginger and mix thoroughly. Place a small amount of the filling on each square of dough. Fold over once to form a triangle and pinch the edges together with the fingertips or floured fork tines. Bake in a greased pan at 400 degrees until golden brown (about 12 minutes). Quickly remove to a bowl and baste several times with honey. Makes about 40.

COCONUT PIROSHKI

4 cups flour
3/4 cup sugar
2 teaspoons baking
  powder
pinch of salt
4 eggs, beaten
1/2 cup oil
1/2 cup water

1 ounce poppy seed
2 cups shredded coconut
2 cups chopped nuts
2 cups raisins
2 cups sugar
1 pint bottle light Karo
  syrup
oil for brushing

Sift together dry ingredients. Make a well in the center and place in it the eggs, oil, and water; mix thoroughly. Knead. The dough should not stick to the hands; if necessary, add more flour. Roll out dough to paper thinness and brush with oil. Sprinkle with poppy seed, coconut, chopped nuts, and raisins.

Roll up two or three times, as for strudel (see page 153), and cut from the sheet of dough. Cut each roll into 3/4–inch slices. Place on a greased pan and bake at 350 degrees until browned (about 35–40 minutes). Add 2 cups sugar to Karo syrup and bring to a rapid boil.

Drop a few piroshki at a time into the boiling syrup (they will break if crowded). Cook until golden brown, 3 to 5 minutes. Remove piroshki to a platter as they are finished. Makes about 80. Piroshki will keep indefinitely.

MOHNELECH

[Poppy–Seed Candy]

1 pound poppy seed   **2 cups chopped nuts**
1/2 cup sugar   **(pecans, preferably)**
2 cups honey

Pour boiling water over poppy seed and let stand overnight. Drain. Pound seeds with a pestle or other heavy instrument for at least 10 minutes. (Large poppy seeds can be run through a food grinder.) Pounding cracks the seeds and releases the flavor. Cook sugar and honey over a low flame until the sugar dissolves.

Add poppy seed and cook until thick, stirring frequently. This may take 30 to 40 minutes. Test by dropping a spoonful on a wet board; if it holds its shape it is ready for the next step. Stir in nuts. Cook 1 minute longer.

Turn out onto a wet wooden board. Dip the hands in ice water and pat the mixture to 1/2–inch thickness. Let cool 5 to 10 minutes. Cut into 1–inch squares with a sharp knife that has been dipped in hot water. Makes about 50 pieces.

BEET EINGEMACHTS

(Preserves)

2 pounds beets
2 pounds sugar
1 tablespoon ginger

3 lemons, sliced
1 cup coarsely chopped
   almonds

Peel and dice beets. Place beets and remaining ingredients in a deep kettle and cook over a moderate flame for 1 hour. Turn into jelly glasses or a small crock. Store in a dark place to prevent loss of color. This is served as a sweet preserve. Makes about 3 jelly glasses.

❤ 19 ❤

STRUDEL COMES BUT ONCE A YEAR

In our home strudel came but once a year. It was baked before Rosh Hashonah and was supposed to last until after Yom Kippur. This is not unusual. A good strudel can keep a long time, and like some people I know, it gets even better with age. The flavors mix up together so you don't know which is which. This was Mama's reward—that no one should be able to guess what was in the strudel!

You don't believe me? You think because you read somewhere in a cookbook what goes into strudel so you know already? Don't be so positive. The next time you eat a piece of strudel, for all you know it may have in it cabbage. Pheh! Not my strudel. But some people do make from cabbage strudel. So don't laugh. Maybe it's good, too, but cabbage strudel I never ate yet and I'm still living.

How can I explain to you the difference in strudel fillings? I'll try to explain with a little art because art, like strudel making, depends on where you are coming from. If I'm seeing a picture from Holland I'm not expecting it should look like a picture from Italy because in Holland is windmills. So I know already if I see a picture with wind-mills it must be Holland, but this does not mean that all the pictures from Holland are the same. No. Some painters are putting in the picture windmills, others are putting in tulips or canals. It depends what the artist likes. The same with strudel. And this is not already the whole answer because if a Dutch painter is coming to New York he would maybe paint tulips on Canal Street, or if he is going to the South he would paint around the windmills magnolia blossoms. I've got a friend, a Southerner, who cooks Loui-siana Gefilte Fish, Creole Style. And sure nough, y'all would go meshugy over it so good it is. The same is also with strudel. Who in Russia has Maraschino cherries? But here you will find in the strudel Maraschino cherries with crushed pineapple yet. And who says it's bad?

So where was I? I was saying strudel will last a long time. I'm not telling a lie. It will last a long time if you keep it in the right place. The best place is a safety deposit box. If you haven't got a safety deposit box, try the highest shelf in the pantry if you've got short children. But if you're living in a modern house and a pantry is already old–fashioned, put the strudel in the built–in bookcase behind the dictionary. The children will never find it there. Or in the piano bench.

In my home we didn't have a dictionary or a piano, so every year I found the strudel. Every year but one. That year Mama switched hiding places in midstream. When I looked in the pantry it was already in the buffet drawer and when I looked in the buffet drawer it was in the oven. When I got around to looking in the oven, it was already back in the pantry and when I found it in the pantry it was already Yom Kippur and on Yom Kippur it's a sin to steal strudel.

It is not, God forbid, like I ate up all the strudel and left nothing for the company after the Yom Kippur fast. I took only one piece at a time ... from the bottom layer, and rearranged the bottom layer so that the few pieces left held up the top layer like a bridge. Came time to serve the company, Mama would moan, "What could happen to the strudel?"

The company would eat and I would watch. "Such strudel," they would say, holding it in one hand and cupping the other hand under they shouldn't lose a crumb. "Such strudel! This is strudel from strudel–land. What did you put in it? If it would be made from gold and silver it wouldn't taste better."

"So eat another piece," Mama would urge. "Can it hurt you?" Them it couldn't hurt. Me it could and did. I would watch them eating the extra pieces, and for what I was thinking better it should have been the eve of the Day of Atonement instead of the eve after.

If the strudel was so good, you're asking, so why did we have it only once a year? Who could afford it more often? Even if you are a millionaire and can afford every day to eat strudel, so who has time to make it? And if you are a millionaire it don't look right you should be in the kitchen. Your cook wouldn't like it. She'd quit. And who can afford to lose a good cook? Where will you find another cook who can make for you a New England boiled dinner or crepes Suzette? So you don't have strudel. But comes a time when you like a piece of strudel. What wouldn't you give for one piece strudel like Mama used to make? Buy it you can't— not with all your millions—so you get yourself invited on a holiday to the home of a Jewish friend. So what happens? Your friend thinks, "The millionaireke is coming to my home. What can I give her that's good enough?" So she runs out to the bakery and buys French pastry. So you see, money isn't everything. It can't buy a good strudel.

To make a good strudel you must have love and patience. You must tenderly roll and pull and stretch the strudel dough until it is so thin you can read through it a Yiddish newspaper—well, anyway the headlines. And don't worry if it don't come out so thin; with all the good things you put in it, what could be bad?

Once you have learned to make a perfect strudel you can stop right there. You've got for yourself already a reputation, because people will think: "If she makes such a good strudel, what can't she make? This is a cook with golden hands!"

APPLE-RAISIN STRUDEL

Dough

5 cups unsifted flour   **1 cup warm water**
3 eggs, slightly beaten

Make a depression in the center of the flour. Slowly add eggs and water. Mix with the hands until the dough leaves the sides of the bowl. This should make a fairly stiff dough that does not stick to the hands. Knead until smooth on a lightly floured white cloth stretched over a pastry board or the kitchen table. Divide the dough into four parts. While working with one part, keep the remainder in a bowl covered with a tea towel to prevent drying. Roll and stretch the dough, turning frequently to form a perfect circle (see directions for stretching noodle dough in "Oodles of Noodles"). Stretch to almost transparent thinness. The thinner the dough, the better the strudel.

Filling

1 scant cup salad oil
1 cup plum preserves
2 1/2 cups finely chop–
   ped nuts
2 1/2 cups fine dry
   bread crumbs*

1 pound seedless raisins
6 cups shredded tart
   apples
1 tablespoon cinnamon
   mixed with 1/2 cup
   sugar

Drop about 2 tablespoons oil on the rolled–out sheet of strudel dough. Using the palm of the hand, spread a thin layer of oil over the entire surface; use more oil if necessary. Drop one fourth of the preserves on the sheet of strudel; spread evenly with the hand. Mix nuts with bread crumbs and sprinkle the mixture evenly over the strudel dough.

Dot with raisins and distribute the shredded apples evenly over the surface. Sprinkle with part of the cinnamon–sugar mix. Roll up tightly three or four times (depending upon the size strudel you want), taking care not to tear the dough.

Cut from remainder of sheet. Lightly oil the top of the roll and sprinkle with cinnamon–sugar mix.

Using a very sharp knife, cut into diagonal slices about 1 1/2 inches wide. Place on shallow, liberally oiled baking tins. Repeat same process with remainder of the dough.

Bake at 350 degrees until lightly browned (about 1 hour). Makes about 70.

*Prepare bread crumbs by baking 10 slices of white bread in a slow oven until lightly browned and very crisp. Grate on a fine grater. It is very important to have crisp, dry bread crumbs.

STRUDEL

Dough

2 1/2 cups sifted flour	**1 tablespoon sugar**
1/2 teaspoon baking powder	**3 eggs, well beaten**
	2 tablespoons oil
1/2 teaspoon salt	**1/4 cup water**

Sift together flour, baking powder, and salt. Stir sugar into beaten eggs. Add oil to water and beat into eggs. Quickly stir the egg–oil mixture into the dry ingredients. Knead in the bowl to a soft dough. Cover bowl with a tea towel and let stand while preparing the filling (recipe follows).

Filling

2 slices crisp toast
1 whole lemon
1 pound nuts (pecans or walnuts)
1 pound dates
1 cup crystallized fruit
1/2 pound white seed–less raisins

oil
6 ounces preserves
shredded coconut
1/2 cup cinnamon–sugar mix (1 tablespoon cinnamon and 1/2 cup sugar)

Put toast, lemon, nuts, dates, crystallized fruit, and raisins through the medium blade of a food grinder. Divide dough into two parts. While working with one part, keep the remainder in a bowl covered with a tea towel to prevent drying.

Place dough on a lightly floured white tablecloth stretched over the kitchen table, and roll and stretch it to paper thinness. (See "Oodles of Noodles" for rolling and stretching directions.)

Brush sheet of dough with oil and spread with preserves. Sprinkle with shredded coconut and ground fruit mixture.

Roll up carefully until half the sheet of dough has been used. Cut away from remainder of sheet. Make a second roll with the remaining half of the sheet. Brush the tops of the rolls with oil and sprinkle with cinnamon–sugar mix.

Repeat this same process with the remainder of the dough. Bake on a well–greased baking tin at 350 degrees until well browned (about 1 hour). Slice while warm. Makes about 36.

Note: Amounts of filling given are approximate. The more expert you become at stretching the dough, the more filling you will need. A friend of mine became so expert at this art that she couldn't afford to make strudel any more.

PINEAPPLE STRUDEL

Dough

5 cups flour
1/4 cup sugar
pinch of salt

3 eggs, beaten
3/4 cup salad oil
1 cup lukewarm water

Sift together flour, sugar, and salt. Add eggs, oil, and water. Mix thoroughly. Cover with a tea towel and let stand while preparing the filling.

Filling

4 cups nuts (pecans or walnuts)
2 pounds pitted dates
3 whole oranges
rind of two lemons
3 or 4 slices crisp toast
1 cup pineapple preserves
1 cup cherry preserves
1 cup plum preserves

2 20 ounce cans crushed pineapple, drained
salad oil
2 cups shredded coconut
cinnamon–sugar mix (1 tablespoon cinnamon and 1 cup sugar)

Put nuts, dates, oranges, and lemon rind through a food grinder. Put enough crisp toast through the grinder to absorb juices. Mix together the preserves and pineapple.

Knead dough for about 5 minutes on a lightly floured pastry board or a white table cloth stretched over the kitchen table. Divide dough into four parts. Work with one part, keeping the remainder in a covered bowl. Roll and stretch the dough to paper thinness (see "Oodles of Noodles" for directions). Brush the sheet of strudel dough with oil. Spread with mixed preserves and sprinkle with shredded coconut. Spread with the ground fruit mixture. Roll up carefully three or more times and cut from the sheet. Continue this process until all the dough has been used. Brush the top of each roll with oil and sprinkle with part of the cinnamon–sugar mix. Cut at 1 1/2–inch intervals. Place on liberally oiled shallow baking tins and bake at 350 degrees until lightly browned (about 45 minutes). Makes about 70.

APPLE STRUDEL

1 1/2 cups flour	1 cup chopped almonds
1/4 teaspoon salt	1 cup seedless raisins
1 egg, slightly beaten	cinnamon–sugar mix (1
1/3 cup warm water	tablespoon cinnamon
1/2 cup melted shortening	to 1 cup sugar)
8 cups shredded apples	shortening

Combine flour, salt, and egg in a large mixing bowl. Add water and mix dough quickly with a knife. Knead on an unfloured board. Stretch dough up and down until it leaves the board clean. Toss onto a well–floured board. Cover with a hot bowl and set in a warm place for 1 hour.

Lay dough in the center of a well–floured tablecloth on the kitchen table; brush with some of the melted shortening. Carefully stretch and pull dough (do not roll) until it is a paper–thin round. Trim edges. Brush with melted shortening. Sprinkle with apples, nuts, raisins, and cinnamon-sugar mix. Dot with shortening. Roll up three or four times, depending upon the size strudel you want, and cut from the remainder of the strudel sheet. Continue the process until all the dough has been used. Place rolls carefully on a well–greased baking tin. Bake at 350 degrees until well browned (about 50 to 60 minutes).

Note: I don't have the courage to try this recipe. If you do, let me know how it comes out.

WALNUT STRUDEL

Dough

3 cups flour	1/2 cup salad oil
1 teaspoon baking	1 egg, beaten
powder	warm water
1/4 teaspoon salt	

Sift together flour, baking powder, and salt. Make a depression in the center of the dry ingredients; place in it the oil and beaten egg. Mix thoroughly. Add only enough warm water to make a "spongy" dough. Cover the bowl with a tea towel and let stand while preparing the filling.

Filling *

1 pound walnut meats, chopped	**3 whole lemons, quartered**
2 heaping teaspoons cinnamon	**3 whole navel oranges, quartered**
1 3/4 cups sugar	**2 slices crisp toast**
1 pound seedless white raisins	**salad oil**
	granulated sugar

Mix chopped nuts with cinnamon and 3/4 cup sugar. Put raisins, toast, lemons, and oranges through a food grinder. Add 1 cup sugar to this mixture.

Divide the dough into four parts. While working with one part, keep the remainder in a bowl covered with a tea towel, to prevent drying.

Place one part on a lightly floured white tablecloth stretched over a pastry board or the kitchen table. Roll and stretch dough (see "Oodles of Noodles") until it is almost transparent. Spread dough with oil and sprinkle with part of the nut–cinnamon–sugar mix.

Starting about 1 inch from edge nearest you, spread a 1–inch line of the ground fruit mixture across the width of the sheet.

Roll up carefully two or three times (depending upon the size strudel you want), and cut from the strudel sheet. Seal cut edge by pressing against the top of the roll. Sprinkle roll with granulated sugar and cut at 1 1/2–inch intervals.

Place pieces carefully on a liberally oiled shallow baking tin. Continue this same process until all the dough has been used. Bake at 350 degrees until well browned (about 45 minutes). Makes about 40.

SOUR CREAM STRUDEL

1/2 pound butter (at room temperature)

1 cup sour cream
2 cups flour

Filling *

2 cups shredded coconut
2 cups chopped nuts

2 cups apricot preserves
powdered sugar

Cream butter. Work in sour cream. Add flour and mix thoroughly with a pastry blender. Wrap in waxed paper and refrigerate overnight.

Divide the dough into eight parts; work with one part at a time, keeping the remainder in the refrigerator. Roll dough to a very thin round on lightly floured waxed paper. Lift and turn circle of dough after every second or third "rolling," reflouring waxed paper each time to keep the dough from sticking. Each section of dough should make a round 12 to 15 inches in diameter. Sprinkle with coconut and chopped nuts. Starting 1 inch from the edge nearest you, spread a straight line of apricot preserves 1 inch wide across the width of the dough.

Roll up carefully by lifting the waxed paper at the edge nearest you. Each time you raise the paper higher, the dough will make another turn. This is as simple as pulling a rug out from under someone. (Try it sometime!) Carefully lift the waxed paper and strudel roll onto a shallow baking tin or cookie sheet, and carefully pull the waxed paper out from under the strudel. Bake at 450 degrees for 10 minutes. Reduce heat to 350 degrees and continue baking until lightly browned (about 25 minutes). Using a sharp knife, slice strudel very carefully at 1 1/2–inch intervals. Sprinkle with powdered sugar when cool. Makes about 50.

NOTE: This strudel should not be as brown as other types of strudel.

KOSHER KOCKT'LS

Times change! You wouldn't believe it how times change. For some people they get better, for some they get worser. If times don't get better or worser, at least they get different. When I was a girl, we lived in a bungalow. When I got married, we lived in an apartment. When the children came, we had a house. When the children married, the house was too big so we sold it. After all when you are *kevetching* in the back, who wants to cut the grass?

So what do we do? We bought a condominium. Did I ever dream I would live in a condominium? Never! I had to celebrate.

So how? Nu? You'll say "Make a party." Naturally, but what kind? They don't have in a book how to make a condominium party.

So I ask the children. "Make a house warming," they tell me. "Have kockt'ls and or derves" ... that's a French word, yet.

Kockt'ls I can't make, but my grandson says he will make and he will tend bar, he calls it. But what will I do. I have never made or derves. Jewish cooking I do, not French. "Cook like you cook," they say, "only make it smaller." So here in this chapter I'm making like a French Jewish cook.

P.S. The housewarming party I'm making was such a success I think I'll make next year another one.

CORNED BEEF BISCUITS

biscuit dough   **chopped corned beef**

Roll biscuit dough to 1/8–inch thickness. Spread with chopped corned beef. Roll as a jelly roll, and slice at 1/4–inch intervals. Bake, cut side down, on a greased cookie sheet in a 450–degree oven for 12 to 15 minutes.

BUTTERFISH SPREAD

1 smoked butterfish (about 1/4 pound) or same amount of whitefish

1/2 pound cream cheese
2 ounces milk or cream (or more)

Remove skin and large bones from fish. Cream together fish and cheese until smooth. Add enough milk or cream to make a smooth spread. This makes about 1 1/2 cups of spread. Add more liquid for a "dip."

CHEESE WAFERS

1 cup prepared biscuit mix
1 cup grated cheese

1/4 teaspoon salt
1/2 cup water

Combine biscuit mix, cheese, and salt; stir in water. Press dough through the small shapes of a cookie press or drop by teaspoonfuls onto an ungreased cookie sheet. Bake at 450 degrees for about 10 minutes. Makes about 60.

CHEESE–NUT BALLS

4 tablespoons flour
1 teaspoon salt
1/4 teaspoon pepper
2 cups grated cheddar
    cheese

2 egg whites, beaten
    until stiff
1/2 cup finely chopped
    nuts
fat for deep–frying

Mix together flour, salt, pepper, and cheese. Fold in egg whites and blend well. Form into small balls. Roll in chopped nuts. Fry in deep hot fat until golden brown (about 1 minute). Makes 40.

LOX PINWHEELS

1/2 pound sliced lox
    (smoked salmon)
3 ounces cream cheese

4 tablespoons milk or
    cream

Spread slices of lox with cream cheese that has been moistened with milk or cream. Roll up as jelly rolls. Wrap in waxed paper and refrigerate until ready to use. Slice crosswise and serve on rounds of toast or crackers.

Note: This makes less than you would like. Condominium parties are so expensive. Better to have a gathering and serve tea with lemon.

PICKELILIES

1 pound salami   sweet pickles

Remove outer skin of salami and slice very thin (about 24 slices). Wrap a slice of salami, calla–lily fashion, around a lengthwise slice of sweet pickle. Fasten with a toothpick.

SWEET AND SOUR MEAT BALLS

Prepare piquant meat balls (see page 53). Form into balls the size of a marble. Cook as directed. Keep hot in a chafing dish.

GEFILTE FISH BALLS

Prepare gefilte fish (see page 80). Form into balls 1/2–inch in diameter. Cook as directed. Serve cold with horseradish.

PIROSHKIS

Prepare piroshki dough (see page 28). Cut into 1 1/2–inch rounds or squares. Fill with meat filling and sprinkle liberally with pepper. Bake as directed. Serve piping hot.

COCKTAIL BLINTZES

Make blintzes (see page 45) in a 6–inch skillet. Cut each blintze into eight pie–shaped wedges (these will be about 2 inches wide at the outer edge). Place 1/2 teaspoon meat filling (see page 46 or 111) at the outer edge and roll as a jelly roll. Skewer with a toothpick. Fry in deep hot fat until lightly browned. Drain quickly on paper toweling and serve hot.

COCKTAIL KNISHES

Prepare knish dough and filling (see page 31). Roll out dough according to directions. Place a line of filling 1/2 inch from the edge nearest you; the filling should be about 1/2 inch wide and 1/2 inch thick. Proceed as in knish recipe, but make smaller.

COCKTAIL SUGGESTIONS

Chopped herring (see page 86). Serve on rounds of toasted rye or pumpernickel bread. Garnish with grated egg yolk.

Chopped liver (see page 77). Serve as a spread on rounds of toasted rye bread. Serve Chopped Liver Strawberries or Pineapple (page 78).

Chopped eggplant (see page 93). Serve on rounds of toasted rye bread. Garnish with grated egg yolk.

How to Pickle a Tongue So It Shouldn't Talk Back

When it comes to how to pickle a tongue so it shouldn't talk back I'm thinking that the best place to go is Greenwald's Super Deluxe Delicatessen because not only is Mr. Greenwald a good tongue pickler, but to him no one would talk back because if you are talking back to him you're getting right away an answer.

You're saying, "Mr. Greenwald, please ... I want a little service."

"So what are you complaining?" he answers back. "You're asking for a little service. So that's what you're getting."

Was a time when Greenwald's was not so super deluxe. The delicatessen was in Louisville on Jefferson Street, like they say, a poor–type neighborhood. And like they say in Yiddish, it was "haimish"—a homelike atmosphere. In other words, a palace it wasn't. So if you think this bothered the Greenwalds so you couldn't be more wrong. On the wall is hanging a sign: GREENWALDS, WALGREENS, WHAT'S THE DIFFERENCE? Also there are signs for the customers: DON'T KNIPE THE BAGEL; DON'T TAHP THE BREAD; SALAMI, A NICKEL A SHTICKEL.

When son David came back from the army, so is added a new sign: WHEN IN INDIA, TRY OUR NEW DEHLI–CATESSEN. You can see that travel broadened David. When I say "broadened" I mean the mind, not the body. Tall he is and thin like a langer lokch (a long noodle) and such a nice Yiddishe face he has that when he was in the service in Japan a Turkish woman took pity on him and cooked for him a Russian dinner.

So what can you do with the young boys when they come back from the service? The old place wasn't good enough for David any more. He wanted a super deluxe delicatessen. So now in the Highlands, a high–class neighborhood, is Greenwald's Delicatessen. A palace it is, not a delicatessen. On the wall is hand–painted a mural, French yet, with in the background the Arc de Triumph. This is expensive—after all, hand–painted—and the upkeep when it has to be painted over is expensive. But David wanted nothing but the best. So you can put the Greenwalds in a palace, but as long as they are running it themselves personal, you still got haimishkeit.

So to Mr. Greenwald I'm going for recipes how to pickle a tongue and make corned beef; how to make pickles and tomatoes and how to stuff a kishke. So I'm calling this chapter "How to Pickle a Tongue," but my first recipe is how to make a corned beef, because, to tell the truth, corned beef I like better.

CORNED BEEF

6 to 8 pounds boneless brisket
1 cup salt
1/2 teaspoon sugar
1 pod garlic, sliced

2 tablespoons mixed pickling spices
1/4 teaspoon saltpeter
pinch of alum

Place brisket in a large stoneware crock and cover completely with water. Add remaining ingredients, stirring to distribute them evenly. Cover meat with an inverted dish weighted down with a heavy stone that has been cleaned thoroughly. Let stand at room temperature for 4 days. Place in the refrigerator for 16 days.

Remove brisket from the crock and place it in a large kettle. Cover with boiling water. Boil for 1 1/2 hours. Turn off heat and let stand in water in which it has cooked for at least 2 hours.

Remove meat to another deep kettle. Place in the sink and let cold water run into the kettle (not directly on the meat) for 1 hour. (This seals in the meat juices.) Remove brisket from water and refrigerate until ready to use. To heat, steam in an improvised double boiler.

Note: Mr. Greenwald says that any housewife who is crazy enough to go to all this trouble when she can buy at Greenwald's fancy new delicatessen is really crazy.

PICKLED TONGUE

Use 3– to 4–pound fresh beef tongue and follow recipe for Corned Beef (see above), but cook 15 minutes longer. Cool in a cold–water bath (as with corned beef). Peel off the skin just before serving.

KOSHER DILL PICKLES

1/2 bushel small, firm cucumbers	1 pound salt (about)
1/2 bunch dried dill	5 pods garlic, sliced
water to cover (about 3 gallons)	1/2 pound mixed pickling spices

Wash cucumbers very carefully, one at a time (any sediment left on cucumbers can spoil the entire batch). Place in a large stoneware crock. Break up dill and place among cucumbers. Make a brine of water, salt, garlic, and spices. (A fresh egg, in the shell, when placed in the water will rise to the surface when the proper amount has been added to the water.) Add brine to cucumbers; they must be entirely covered with the liquid.

Cover cucumbers with an inverted dish weighted down with a clean, heavy stone. Let stand at room temperature until done to your liking. The length of time will depend on the room temperature. Pickles may be eaten after the third or fourth day, but well–done pickles must stand a week or longer. When pickles are to your taste, refrigerate them to halt the pickling process. Makes about 10 quarts.

NOTE: This recipe gives minimum amounts of dill and garlic. More can be added, to taste.

KOSHER DILL PICKLES, CANNED

1 bushel small, firm cucumbers	1/4 pound mixed pickling spices
1/2 bunch dried dill	1 3/4 pounds salt
10 pods garlic, sliced	5 gallons water (about)

Sterilize jars. Wash cucumbers carefully, one at a time, and place in the jars. Break up dill and distribute equally among the jars. Add equal amounts of garlic and spices to each jar.

Dissolve salt in water; fill jars to the top with this brine solution. Seal tightly. Immerse jars in very hot water for 2 or 3 minutes; this helps seal them tightly. Leave in a cool, dark place until done. In very hot weather this may take only 3 days, but in cooler weather it may take as long as a week. Pickles are "done" when their color has changed from a bright cucumber green to a dull, yellowish pickle green. Makes about 20 quarts.

PICKLED GREEN TOMATOES

Follow recipe for Kosher Dill Pickles on page 168, using 1/2 bushel small, firm green tomatoes in place of cucumbers, and omitting dill.

♥ 22 ♥

So Why Should You Kill Yourself? Or Short Cuts

Before I'm answering the question why should you kill yourself, I'm doing a lot of thinking on the subject because when you are writing a book so you have to give reasons. I can't just say why should you kill yourself; I've got to give an answer pro and con. So while I'm thinking on this subject, I'm thinking about the old–fashioned Jewish cook. Now, the old–fashioned Jewish cook thinks if she doesn't spend the whole day in the kitchen so how can it be good? The young cook is different. Here is everything push–a–

button, hurry–up, do it the quick and easy way so you should have time to go to a Sisterhood meeting or to spend the day at child–psychology classes to learn how to make your child emotionally secure so it shouldn't grow up like a bum on the street.

So the question is this: How can you cook something good and not kill yourself in the kitchen all day? This is not an easy question.

One day a friend is giving me a recipe how to cook praakes (rolled cabbage) in a pressure cooker, one–two–three. Right away I think this is the answer and I begin to collect recipes how to cook quick and good. For years I'm collecting, so what have I got? I've got a recipe how to cook praakes in a pressure cooker you should put in only a bottle of catsup, and a recipe how to make pickled beets you should just open up a can and put in a little juice from sweet pickles, and this is all.

I'm more modern now. I don't cook from a pressure cooker. I am almost modern enough to cook from a micro-wave. No, I did that, but I like better to cook like Mama did, so the meat should get brown and the flavors should mix like in *Love and Knishes*. So keep with you the book.

Index